PETROS DRAGOUMIS

THE 6 STRING BASS GUITAR

MODE SYSTEM CONCEPT

VOLUME 1 : MAJOR MODES

A comprehensive analysis and application of the modal system, and practical learning techniques for the entire fingerboard through the study of modes, scales, intervals, chords, and their respective diagrams

ISBN-13: 978-1-949880-00-7

Copyright © 2018 by Petros Dragoumis.

All Rights Reserved

Published 2018 by Odeion Books , Chicago, Illinois.

to Jaco

CONTENTS

Contents

INTRODUCTION

The series of books for learning the Bass Guitar with the **mode system concept** is based on the processing and the geometrical structure and coexistence of the modes in every key. The system begins with the mother scales, the principal scales that exist in the western musical system. Those are the **major scale**, the **harmonic minor scale**, and the **melodic minor scale**. We do not mention the **natural minor scale** as a mother scale because its construction is covered during the studies of the major scale in which we find the natural minor as its 6th mode, known as the Aeolian mode.

When we look at each mother scale, we find the modes that are built on each scale degree, and we study them through a specific shape pattern, harmonization, and most importantly specific fingering positions. The most essential point is that with this system we have to maintain a very specific **fingering pattern** for each mode, so that the movement becomes consistent and automatic through our fingers but also our brain, which leads to flexible and effortless playing. With every mode, we first learn its shape on one octave with specific fingerings, and by studying the exercises included in this book we are able to establish its geometrical pattern. In addition, through the continuous repetition that the exercises demand, we are able to own its melodic presence.

We also find all the **intervals** that are formed on all the scale degrees of each mode which are based on the tonic note, and as a result we learn the character and the sound quality they create within the environment of each mode.

Consequently, we harmonize each mode, which means that we find the **triad** and **7th chord** that are created through the vertical positioning of the scale degrees, which is based on intervals of thirds. That is how we find the triad of the 1st, 3rd, and 5th scale degrees of each mode, as well as the seventh chord by adding the 7th degree of the mode.

This is how we complete the detailed research of each mode while building the basis for the further study of the entire system.

Once we have thoroughly learned in chapter 1 each mode separately, in chapter 2 we find its placement as part of the key where it belongs, establishing its place (scale degree), and from there we study and learn the modes as scale degrees of the mother scale. We construct the **modes horizontally**, one scale degree after another, in order, as well as their **diatonic chords and arpeggios**, and that way we establish the entire key center on the fingerboard by learning it as a combined group of notes.

The next stage in chapter 3 is the vertical positioning of the modes on the fingerboard, by finding each mode that is on top or below another mode, and by following the geometry of the instrument. This gives us the ability, by applying the fingering and geometry that we learned in the previous chapters, to comfortably construct the key center vertically. At this point we will also comprehend the meaning behind the **specific fingering** that the system required in the initial chapters, which will offer us the ability to easily and comfortably play the modes in a vertical manner.

Based on the placement of all vertical ways of combinations of the modes, we find **5 vertical positions** on our fingerboard through which we construct fully each key center while at the same time exploring every angle of our instrument.

Continuing, in chapter 4, through those vertical positions we study all the modes arpeggio, inversions, etc. that derive from the key center, and as a result, by combining all 5 positions we will be able to play both melodically and harmonically any key center on the entire length and width of our fingerboard.

in chapter 5, we study all the chord structures that derive from any of the 5 vertical positions separately.

In chapter 6 we find the complete structure of each key center through the 5 vertical positions. Those positions have a repeated pattern on the fingerboard, meaning that each key center begins with a specific position, and once we have played all of them following the order of the numbers, they start all over from the beginning in a circular manner, and they finish where the fingerboard ends.

In chapter 7, we figure out through the tetrachords of the modes how we can play each mode on the fingerboard **diagonally** in 3 octaves, by moving from one string to the next while following the progression order of the tetrachords.

Finaly in chapter 8 we find out how we can use in melodical way the structure of the modes, using as starting point just two notes of the system, **the F and the F♯**.

By the end of the book we get to the point where we can expand on every key center horizontally, vertically, and diagonally, throughout the length and width of the fingerboard. Once we have completed the system, and through the automatic use of the various fingering positions and the geometrical correlation of the various modes, we are able to express ourselves both melodically and harmonically, and to follow the progression of any musical piece, no matter how difficult it is, with comfort and ease.

The **whole system concept** covers the modes of all the mother scales, and due to the volume of the material, it is necessary to create a series of books with each one of them covering the study of a specific mother scale. With this in mind, Volume 1 covers Major and Natural minor modes, Volume 2 covers Harmonic minor modes, Volume 3 covers Melodic minor modes, and finally Volume 4 covers all the Symmetrical and Pentatonic scales.

STUDY GUIDE

While studying this book, students need to follow precisely the structure of each exercise. The exercises are written based on the classical way of teaching, and through multiple repetitions they give the student the ability to overcome any difficult passages.

Once we understand the complete system, we will find that we do not need to learn each mode/scale with the different finger positions, because the geometrical shapes and patterns that exist among them allows us to play them spontaneously and without much thought. We will be surprised to find out what I like to call the **"secret"** scales, chords, and finger positions, and we will discover that if we follow the guidelines of the book, we have already learned them without separate effort for each one. The **mode system concept** includes all the necessary elements that are required for a strong, comprehensive, and complete program of studies for learning Bass guitar, as well as all other string instruments, combined with the fundamentals of music theory.

When a student studies one key center, he or she also learns the structure of other key centers. This occurs because each mode of a specific key center can become the tonic, and the rest become its satellite scale degrees. For example, in the key of C, during the initial development of the key center, the C Ionian mode is the mother scale and the main scale degree of the key center. At the same time, we could replace the main scale degree with the A Aeolian mode, and a musical piece could similarly be based on the Aeolian mode. We could also have as the main scale degree the E Phrygian mode. All of the above are scale degrees of the major scale we have studied, and by using the same automatic fingering that we use with a major key center, we can play any other key center that derives from any of its modes with the same ease.

Due to the volume of the detailed structure of each exercise, it is not feasible to present them in all the key centers, which would require many more books. Therefore, the students have to transfer each exercise to all 12 key centers on their own.

I wish you the best in your studies and application of your knowledge throughout your musical journey.

Petros Dragoumis

CHAPTER 1

Mode Studies

In the first chapter we will examine and study the modes of the major scale.

MODAL SYSTEM

Modal System is called a group of rules that examines the creation of key centers related to specific scales of our music system. Each scale that we know can be inverted into new scales, as many as the number of notes of our original scale. This is how it works: by raising each time the tonic note an octave higher, the subsequent note of our previous scale becomes the next tonic, and this process repeats until the last note of our initial scale becomes the tonic. Therefore, we have as many inversions as the number of notes of our initial scale. Each note of a scale creates its own new scale, and that note becomes the tonic of the new scale. The scales that are created from the inverted scale degrees of a mother scale are called Modes, and we study this inversion and creation process in this chapter.

On the following pages we can see the inversion of the major scale into seven new scales, each of which begins on one of the scale degrees of the major scale. What all those scales have in common is that they use the notes of the major scale, which is also called Ionian, but each one uses the notes in a different order. Each one of those scales has its own tone color, its own musical environment, it creates its own chords, and, in general, it functions in an entirely autonomous way even though it ultimately belongs to the mother major scale. Each mode has its own pattern since the half and whole steps appear in a different order, and the result is a different sound, which is why we need to be able to recognize the modes by their sound quality. In addition, each mode builds its own chord from the 1st, 3rd, 5th, and 7th degrees. Therefore, we have seven chords that derive from the seven modes of the major scale. Those are called diatonic chords, which means that they all belong to the tonality of the mother scale. The modes of the major scale have been given names from the Ancient Greek language since they originated from the modes that the Ancient Greeks used, but with a different order.

TETRACHORDS

Before we move on to the study of the modes, we will examine how tetrachords are built, which are historically the foundation for building scales of all musical systems.

Tetrachords exist in the construction of music since ancient times on all the musical systems, in Ancient Greece in descending form, and in Rome in ascending form. In traditional Middle Eastern music we have the **makam** which are developed both in tetrachords and pentachords, and in traditional Indian music we have the **ragas**. Each major scale involves two tetrachords. This is the case for all 7-note scales as well as their modes that we are going to come across in this book. Therefore, depending on its pattern of intervals, each tetrachord has a certain name which determines the sound quality that it represents. Let's look at the names of the tetrachords in order to be able to identify them in the development of the scales in subsequent chapters.

Major tetrachord, W-W-H: It is called major because it contains a major 3rd and it is the first tetrachord of the major scale.

Minor tetrachord, W-H-W: It is called minor because it contains a minor 3rd and it is the first tetrachord of the natural minor scale.

Phrygian tetrachord, H-W-W: It is called Phrygian because it contains a minor 2nd and a minor 3rd and it is the first tetrachord of the Phrygian mode.

Lydian tetrachord, W-W-W: It is called Lydian because it contains an augmented 4th which we find in the first tetrachord of the Lydian mode.

CONTENT OF EXERCISES

With each mode that we examine, we will first look at its basic construction on the fingerboard of the Bass guitar.
We will find the tetrachords that each mode contains.
We will find the intervals between the tonic and each scale degree of every mode.
We will construct the triad and the 7th chord that are formed from each scale degree of every mode by using the 1st, 3rd, 5th, and 7th note of the mode.

TIPS FOR STUDYING

During the first 6 exercises of each mode and for space efficiency, we show only the beginning and the direction of each exercise.

On each of those exercises we move chromatically on our fingerboard starting on the lowest possible position for forming each mode, and ending on the highest possible position. This means that we will first play each mode exactly how it appears on the exercise, and then we will move it over by a half step, and we will keep repeating that until we run out of room on our fingerboard.

When we get to the highest position where we can play each exercise, we start to move in reverse by moving the exercise half a step back each time, and we repeat that until we run out of room on our fingerboard.

Each time that we move chromatically to a new position, we name the first note of the exercise, which is our new tonic. When we ascend on our fingerboard towards the higher area, we indicate any accidentals with sharps, while when we are descending we indicate them with flats.

Following the above, we have a segment with 9 different melodic exercises which will help us learn how to use each mode in a melodic way. We need to apply each of those exercises to all 12 tonalities of tonal system.

Afterwards, we move on to the block of exercises for triads and 7th chords, with all the possible combinations among all scale degrees. We still need to transfer each exercise to all tonalities.

Finally, we learn all the intervals that are formed between the tonic and each scale degree, as well as the chords that derive from each mode.

As we already mentioned, each exercise should be played on all 12 tonalities using the circle of fifths by moving in perfect fourths each time we go to the next tonality. After we have played them all, we move on to the next exercise. We will not gain much if we only play each exercise once and then rush on to the next because we will not accomplish the knowledge that this book has to offer.

Ionian

- 1st mode of the Major scale
- General formula: W-W-H-W-W-W-H
- Scale: Major with a major seventh
- Tetrachords: major – major
- Characteristic note of the mode: the major 7
- The intervals that are formed between the tonic and each scale degree:
- I-II = 2, I-III = 3, I-IV = 4, I- V = 5, I-VI = 6, I-VII = 7
- The diatonic half steps are found on the scale degrees III-IV and VII-I
- Triad: Major, I
- Seventh chord: Major-major 7, Imaj7, IΔ7, I Δ, I(maj7)
- Extensions: 9, 13
- Generally: The Ionian mode is the natural major scale and from its notes we form the remaining 7 modes of the key center. It is therefore a mother scale. It is a seven-tone scale with a balanced sound. The 4th degree is used melodically only on weak beats as a passing tone because an extended sound could ruin the stability of the sound of the tonic scale.

IONIAN MODE

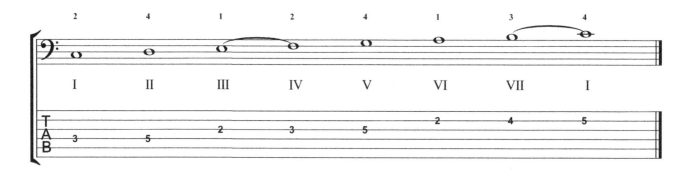

TETRACHORDS

Chapter 1

Ionian mode Intervals

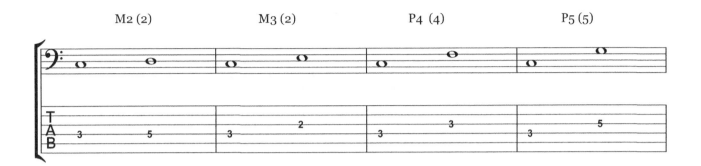

Chords and arpeggios of Ionian Mode

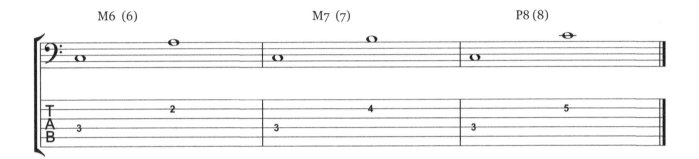

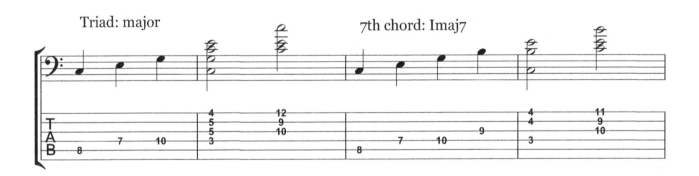

Ionian mode studies

mode exercises

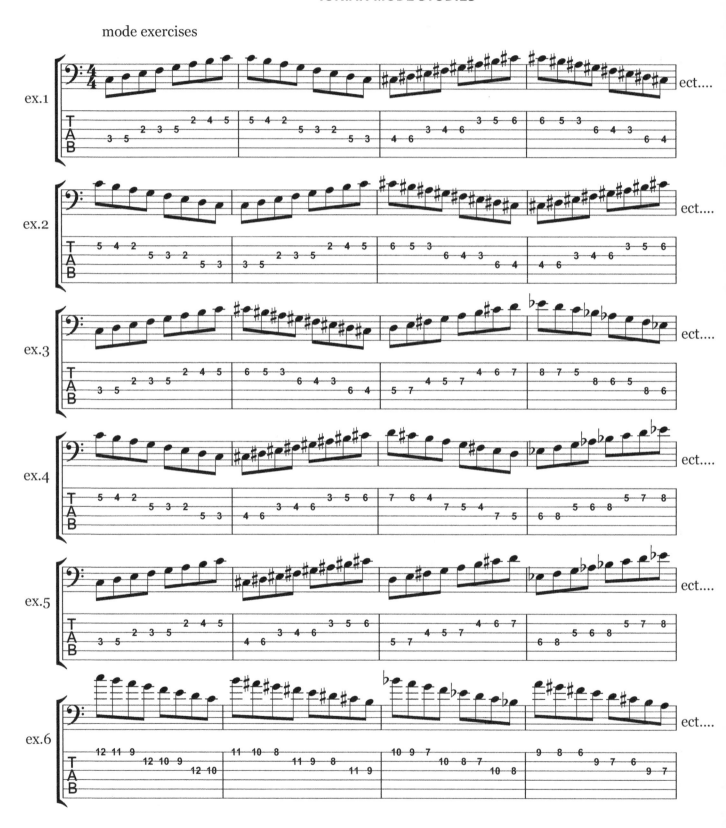

melodic exercises

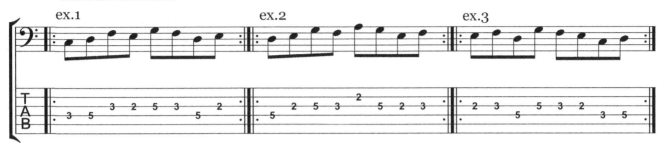

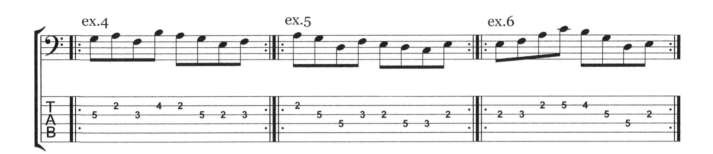

triad exercises

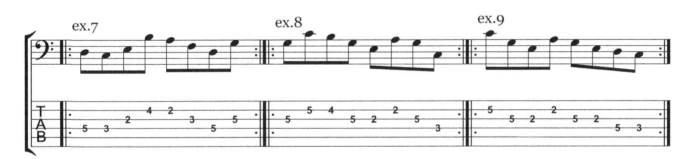

7th chord exercises

ex.16 ex.17 ex.18

ex.19 ex.20 ex.21

ex.22 ex.23 ex.24

Intervals

Chords

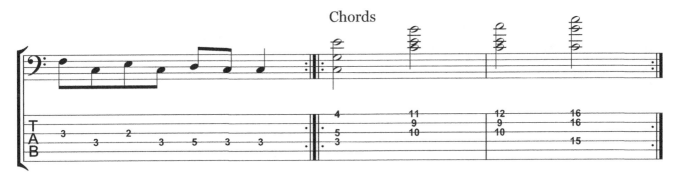

Dorian

- 2nd mode of the Major scale
- General formula: W-H-W-W-W-H-W
- Scale: Minor with a major sixth
- Tetrachords: minor - minor
- Characteristic note of the mode: the major 6
- The intervals that are formed between the tonic and each scale degree:
- I-II = 2, I-III = ♭3, I-IV = 4, I-V = 5, I-VI = 6, I-VII = ♭7
- The diatonic half steps are found on the scale degrees II-III and VI-VII
- Triad: Minor, ii-
- Seventh chord: Minor 7th, ii-7
- Extensions: 9, 11, 13
- Generally: The Dorian mode is the second degree of the mother major. It is a minor scale because it has a minor third in its structure, but it has a major sixth as opposed to the minor scales which usually have a minor sixth. The major sixth gives it an edgier sound similar to the major tone color, and for that reason the Dorian mode is often called jazz minor and is the first choice to play over min6 and min7 chords.

DORIAN MODE

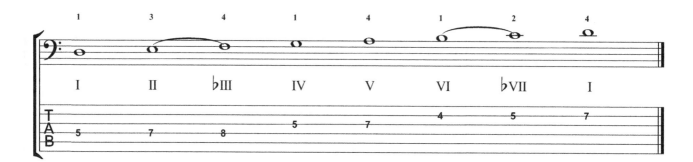

TETRACHORDS

Dorian mode Intervals

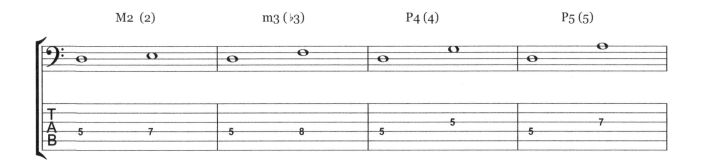

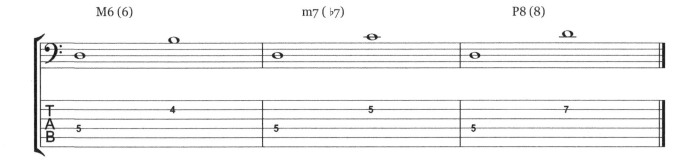

Chords and arpeggios of Dorian Mode

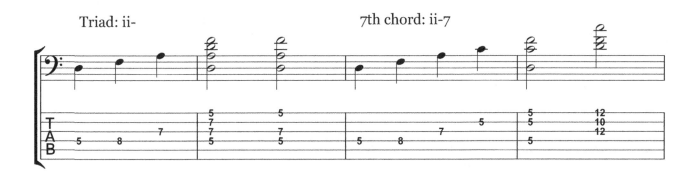

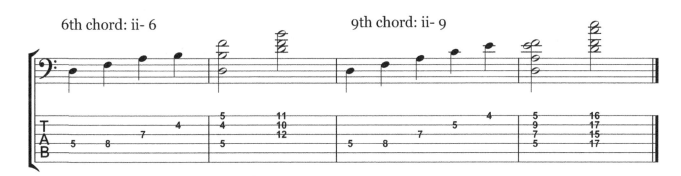

DORIAN MODE STUDIES

mode exercises

melodic exercises

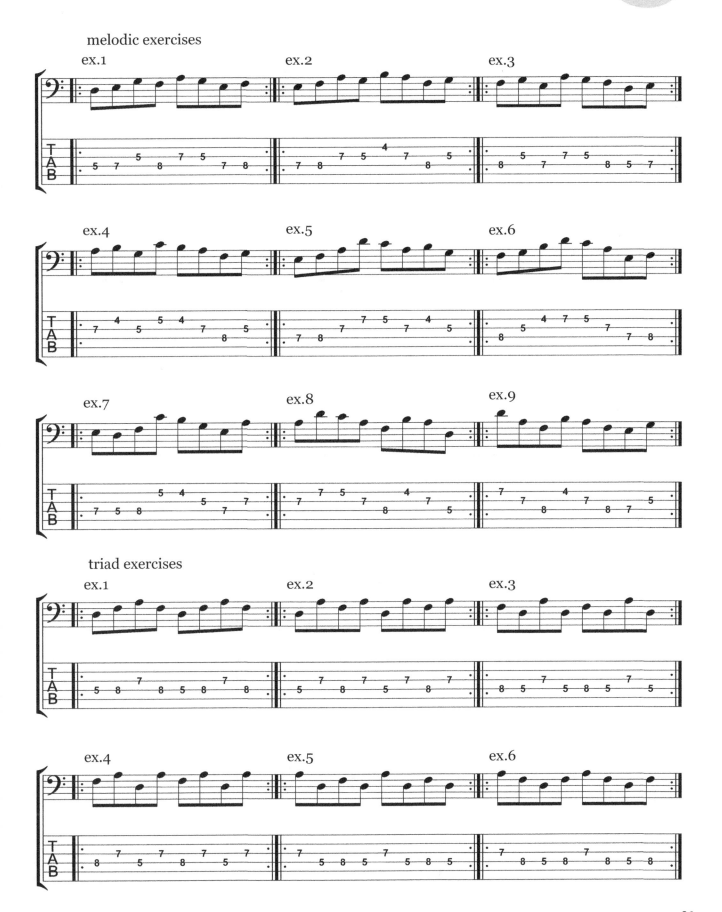

7th chord exercises

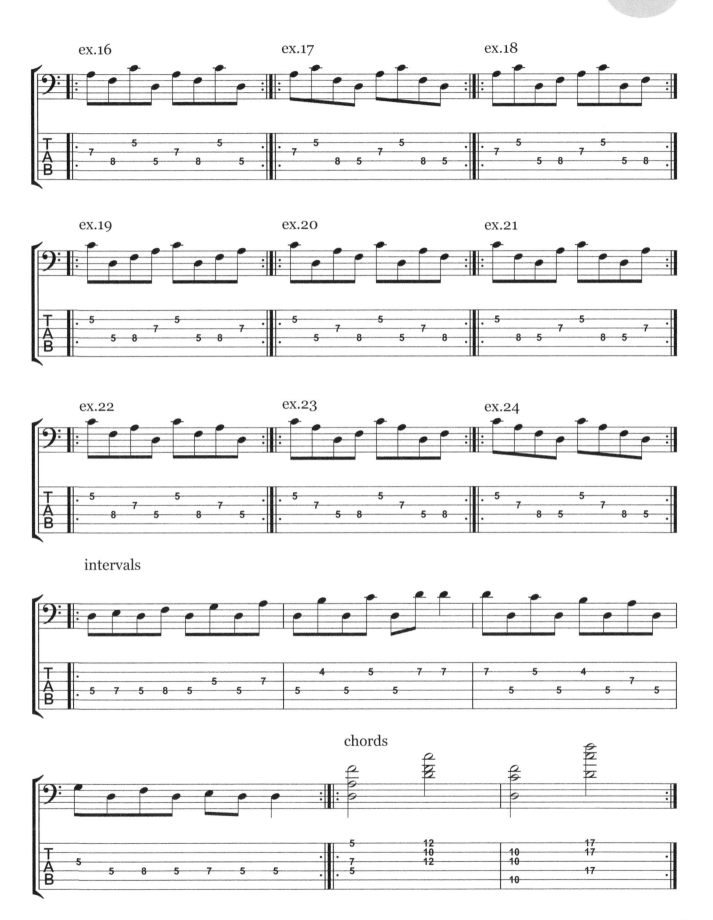

intervals

chords

Phrygian

- 3rd mode of the Major scale
- General formula: H-W-W-W-H-W-W
- Scale: Minor seventh with a minor second
- Tetrachords: phrygian - phrygian
- Characteristic note of the mode: the minor second ♭2
- The intervals that are formed between the tonic and each scale degree:
- I-II = ♭2, I-III =♭3, I-IV = 4, I-V = 5, I-VI = ♭6, I-VII =♭7
- The diatonic half steps are found on the scale degrees I-II and V-VII
- Triad: Minor, iii-
- Seventh chord: Minor 7th, iii-7
- Extensions: 11
- Generally: The Phrygian mode is also a minor scale because it contains a minor third, but the note that distinguishes it is its minor second. This scale is used a lot in Middle Eastern music as well as in Greek music.

PHRYGIAN MODE

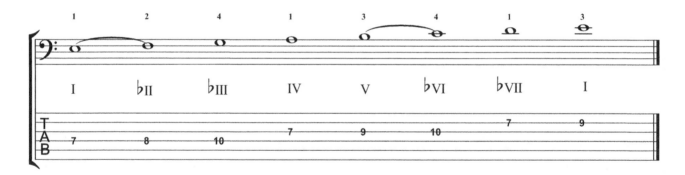

TETRACHORDS

PHRYGIAN MODE INTERVALS

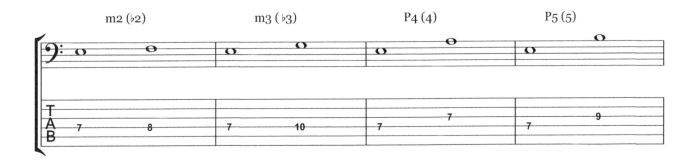

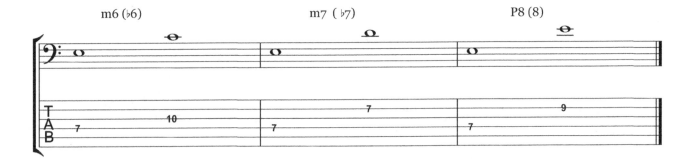

CHORDS AND ARPEGGIOS OF PHRYGIAN MODE

PHRYGIAN MODE STUDIES

mode exercises

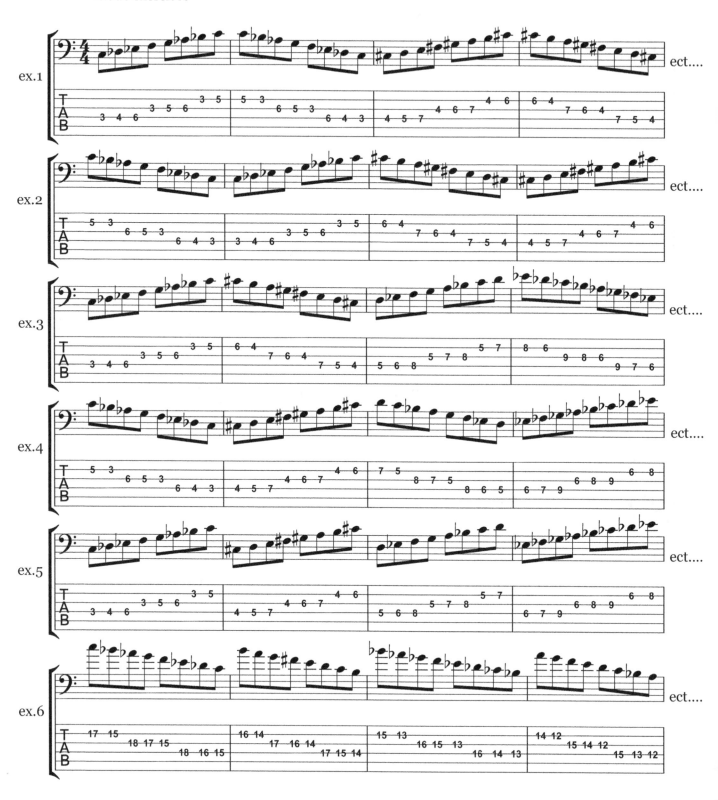

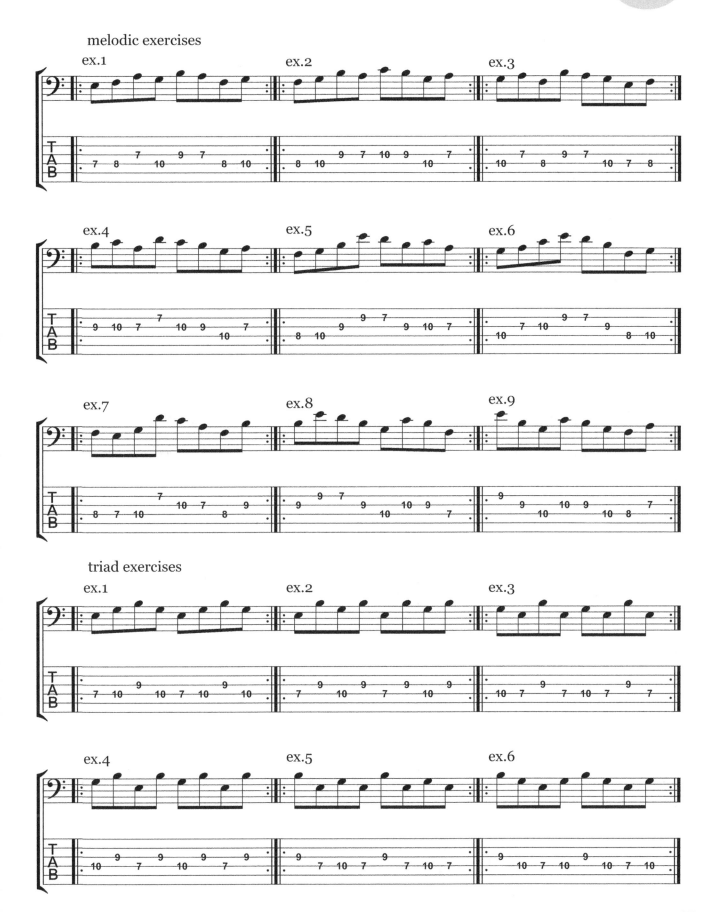

melodic exercises

triad exercises

7th chord exercises

Lydian

- 4th mode of the Major scale
- General formula: W-W-W-H-W-W-H
- Scale: Major seventh with an augmented fourth
- Tetrachords: lydian - major
- Characteristic note of the mode: the augmented fourth ♯4
- The intervals that are formed between the tonic and each scale degree:
- I-II = 2, I-III = 3, I-IV = ♯4, I-V = 5, I-VI = 6, I-VII = 7
- The diatonic half steps are found on the scale degrees IV-V and VII-I
- Triad: Major, IV
- Seventh chord: Major-major 7, IVmaj7, IV Δ7, IVM7
- Extensions: 9, ♯11, 13
- Generally: The Lydian mode is a major scale because it contains a major third, but its characteristic note is the augmented fourth which gives it a "grayish" sound, and therefore, it is used in jazz music as a first choice in major chords with a major 7 instead of the Ionian mode.

Lydian mode

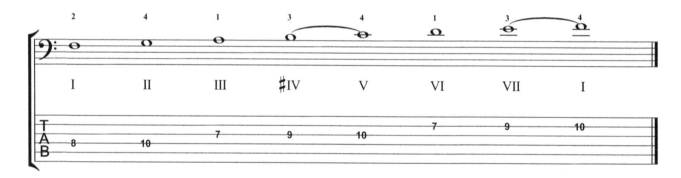

Tetrachords

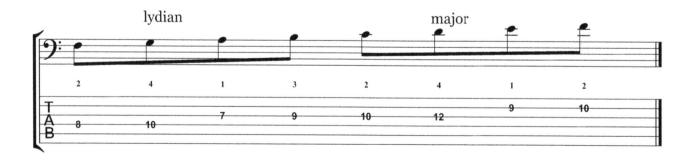

Lydian mode Intervals

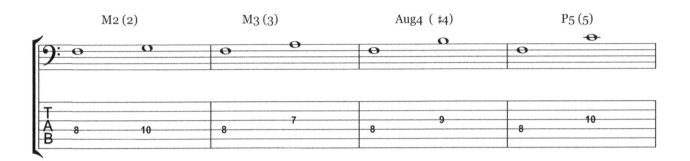

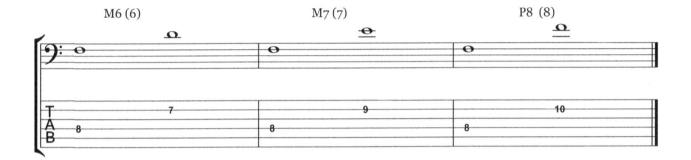

Chords and arpeggios of Lydian Mode

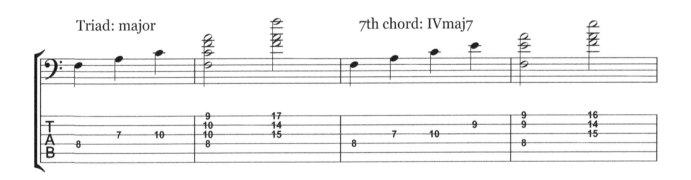

LYDIAN MODE STUDIES

mode exercises

7th chord exercises

Mixolydian

- 5th mode of the Major scale
- General formula: W-W-H-W-W-H-W
- Scale: Major-minor seventh
- Tetrachords: major - minor
- Characteristic note of the mode: the minor seventh ♭7
- The intervals that are formed between the tonic and each scale degree:
- I-II = 2, I-III = 3, I-IV = 4, I-V = 5, I-VI = 6, I-VII =♭7
- The diatonic half steps are found on the scale degrees III-IV and VI-VII
- Triad: Major, V
- Seventh chord: Major 7, V7, Vdom
- Extensions: 9, 13
- Generally: The Mixolydian mode is a major scale because it contains a major third, and its characteristic note is a minor seventh, as opposed to the other two major modes, the Ionian and the Lydian, which contain a major seventh. It is used over chords of V, and it gives a more "blues" tone color.

MIXOLYDIAN MODE

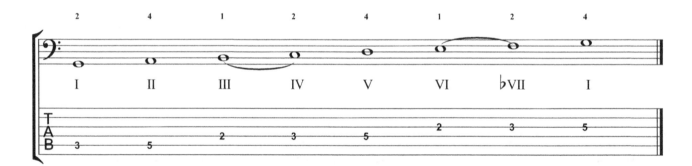

TETRACHORDS

MIXOLYDIAN MODE INTERVALS

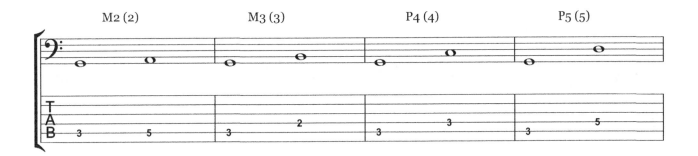

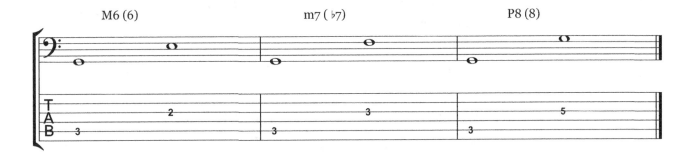

CHORDS AND ARPEGGIOS OF MIXOLYDIAN MODE

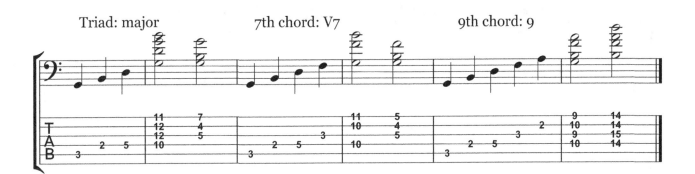

MIXOLYDIAN MODE STUDIES

mode exercises

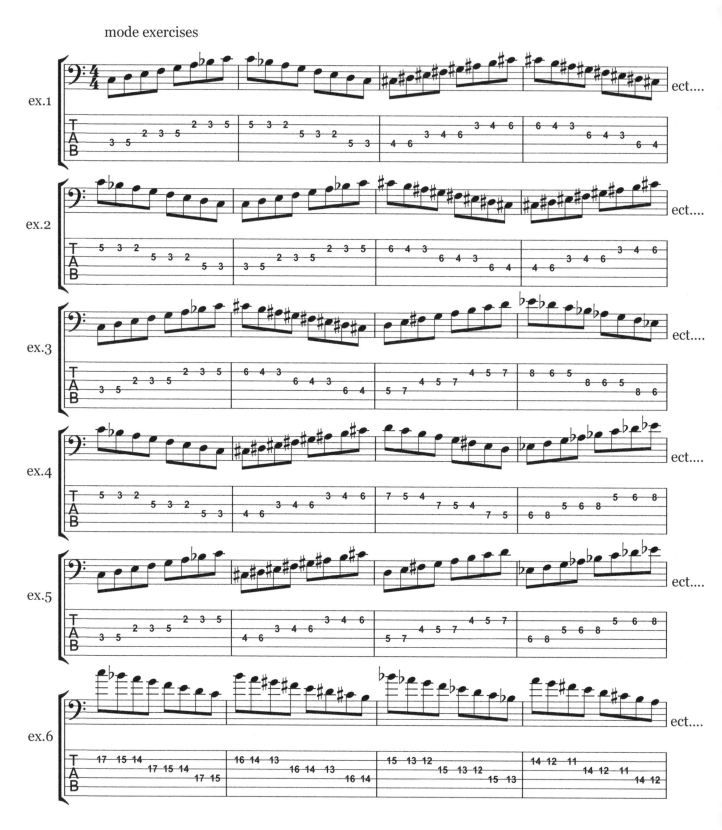

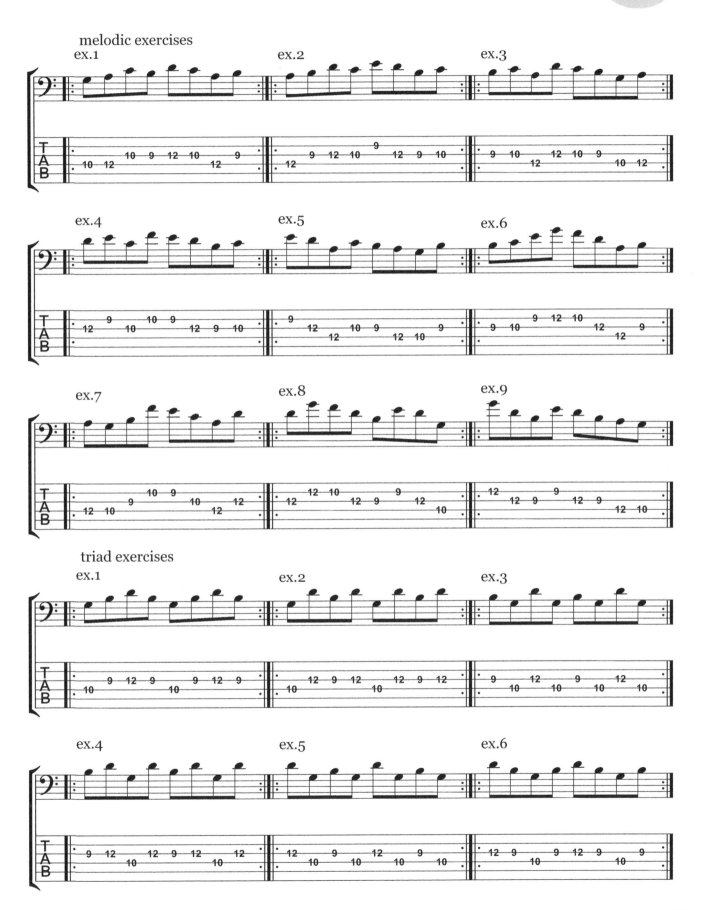

7th chord exercises

Aeolian

- 6th mode of the Major scale
- General formula: W-H-W-W-H-W-W
- Scale: Minor seventh (Natural minor)
- Tetrachords: minor - phrygian
- Characteristic note of the mode: the minor third ♭3
- The intervals that are formed between the tonic and each scale degree:
- I-II = 2, I-III = ♭3, I-IV = 4, I-V = 5, I-VI = ♭6, I-VII = ♭7
- The diatonic half steps are found on the scale degrees II-III and V-VI
- Triad: Minor, vi-
- Seventh chord: Minor 7th, vi-7
- Extensions: 9, 11
- Generally: The Aeolian mode is the Natural minor scale. It has a balanced sound as far as its structure, and it is a point of reference and comparison for the other minor modes of the system. It is also called the relative minor of the mother Major scale.

AEOLIAN MODE

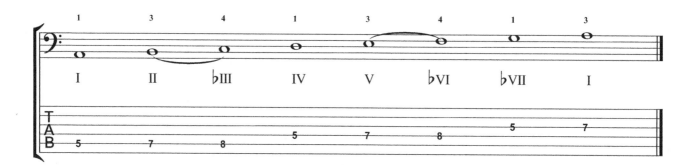

TETRACHORDS

Aeolian mode Intervals

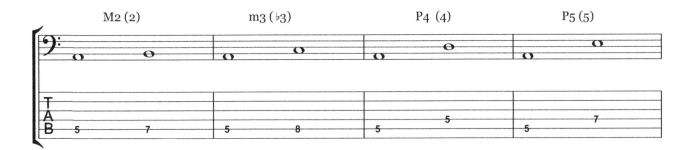

Chords and arpeggios of Aeolian Mode

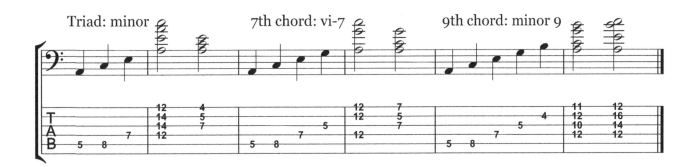

AEOLIAN MODE STUDIES

mode exercises

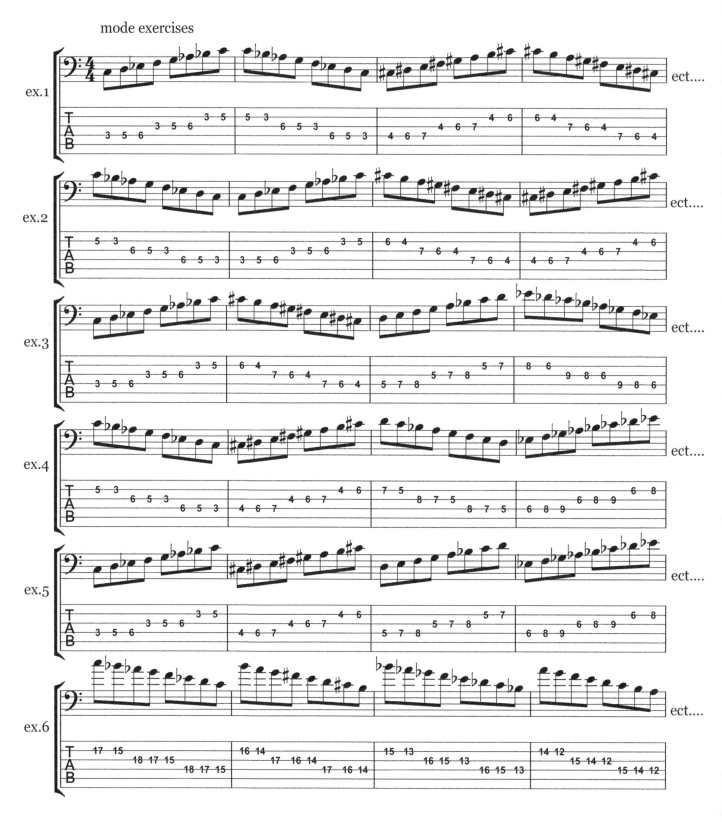

melodic exercises

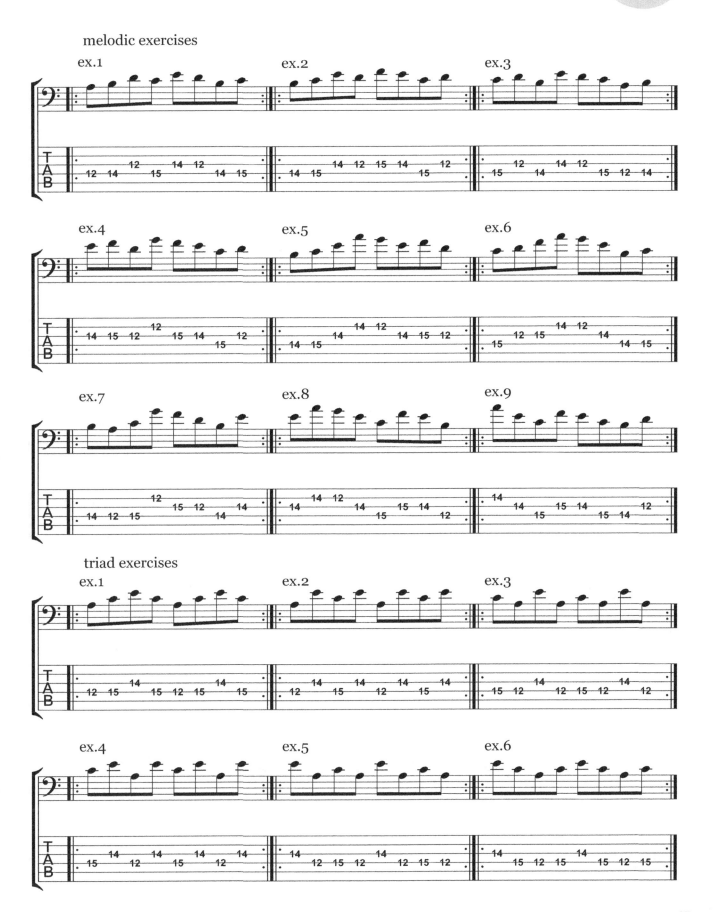

triad exercises

7th chord exercises

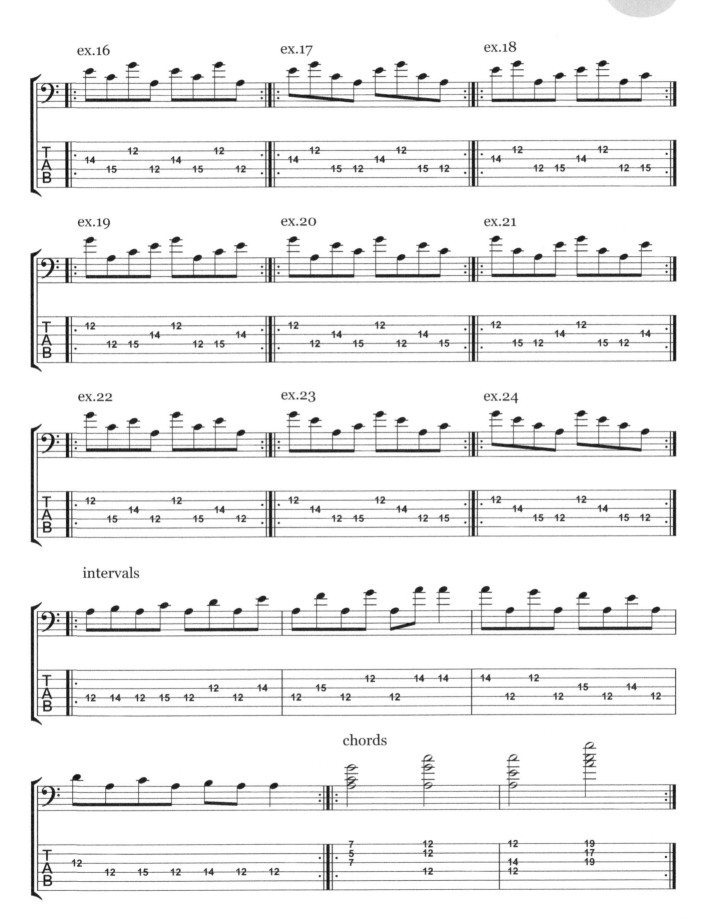

Locrian

- 7th mode of the Major scale
- General formula: H-W-W-H-W-W-W
- Scale: Half-diminished
- Tetrachords: phrygian - lydian
- Characteristic note of the mode: the diminished fifth ♭5
- The intervals that are formed between the tonic and each scale degree:
- I-II = ♭2, I-III = ♭3, I-IV = 4, I-V = ♭5, I-VI = ♭6, I-VII = ♭7
- The diatonic half steps are found on the scale degrees I-II and IV-V
- Triad: Diminished, viio
- Seventh chord: Minor 7th with ♭5, vii-7 (♭5)
- Extensions: ♭13
- Generally: The Locrian mode is a scale that has its own unique sound color. That happens because it contains a minor third and therefore is considered a minor scale, but it also contains a ♭5 which gives it a different sound from the minor scales that we have examined so far. In addition, it contains a ♭9 which gives it an even more unique sound. It is commonly used in the harmonic progression ii-7(♭5) - V7 - i-7.

LOCRIAN MODE

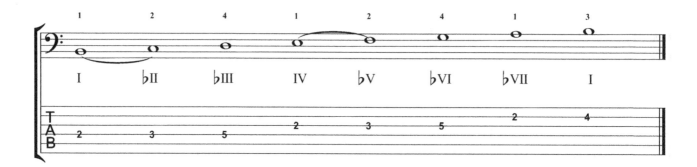

TETRACHORDS

Locrian mode Intervals

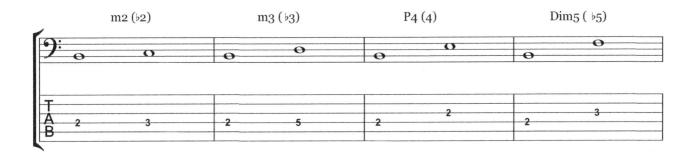

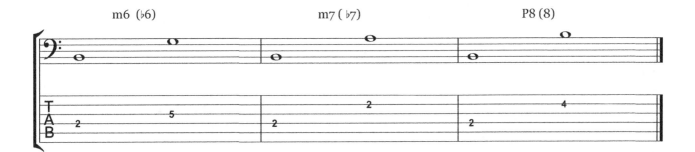

Chords and arpeggios of Locrian Mode

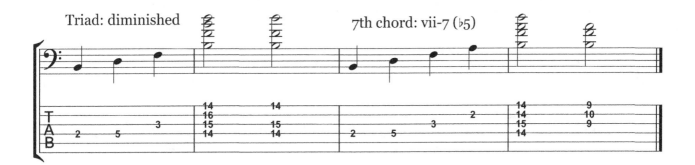

LOCRIAN MODE STUDIES

mode exercises

melodic exercises

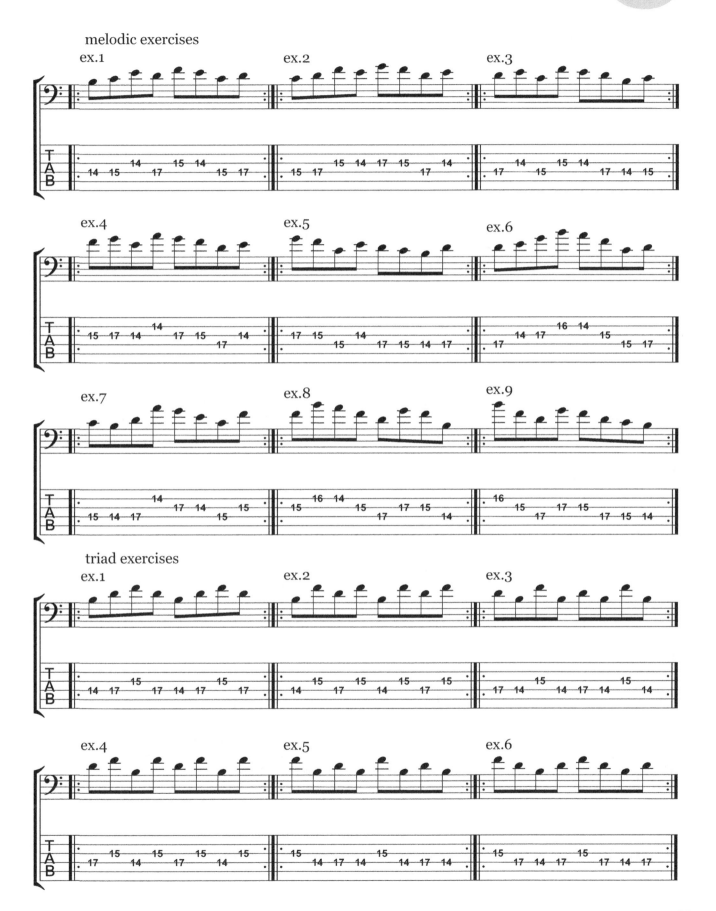

triad exercises

7th chord exercises

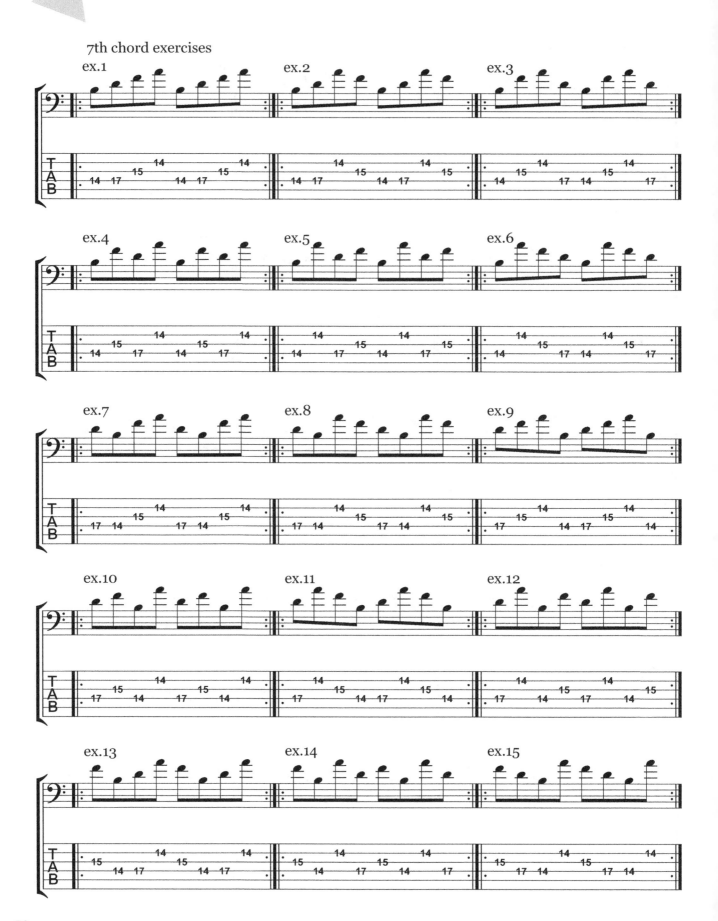

Volume 1: Major modes

Chapter 1

53

CHAPTER 2:

Horizontal structure of the modes

In this chapter we will study how the 7 modes of each mother scale are constructed by placing each one on the respective scale degree it represents in horizontal order on the fingerboard. That way, the progression of the exercise includes sub-parts of study which present the complete structure of the modes and the diatonic chords of the key center.

Study guidelines for this chapter:

There are repeat signs that separate each part of the exercise from the next part.
You should play each exercise part several times before moving on to the next part.
At the end, you should play the entire exercise without the repeats.

C major key modes horizontal studies

diatonic modes exercise 1

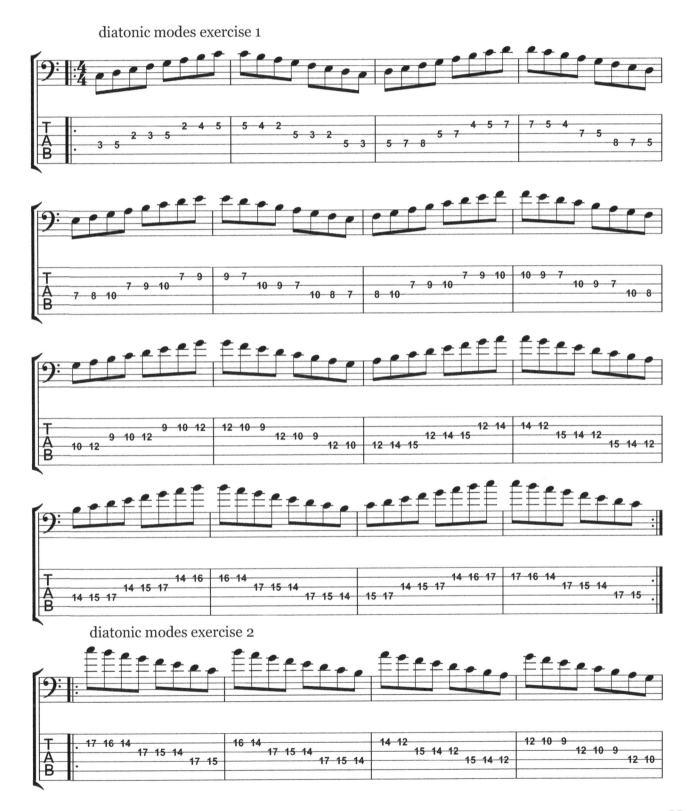

diatonic modes exercise 2

diatonic modes exercise 3

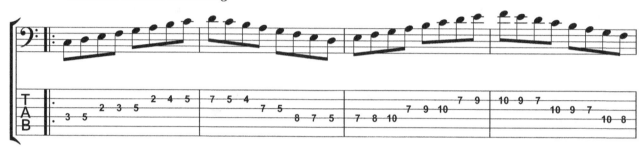

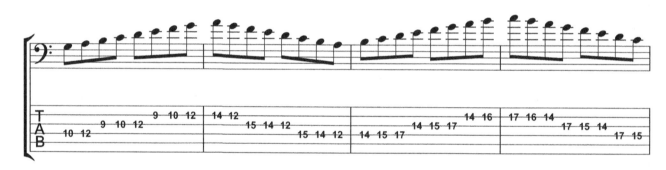

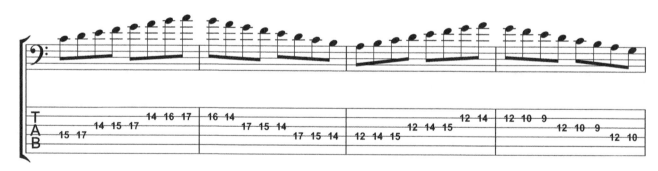

diatonic modes exercise 4

diatonic modes exercise 5

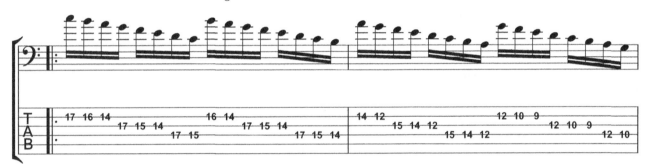

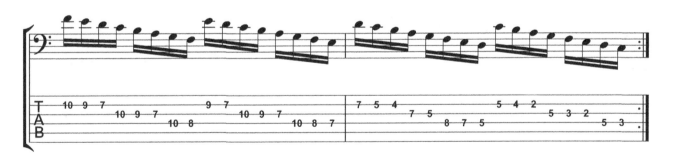

diatonic 7th chords exercise 1

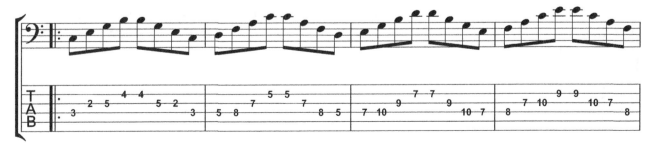

diatonic 7th chords exercise 2

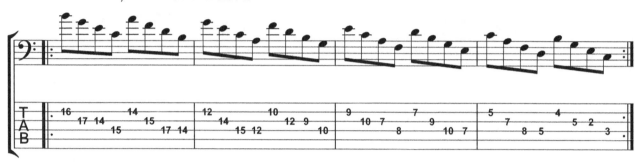

diatonic 7th chords exercise 3

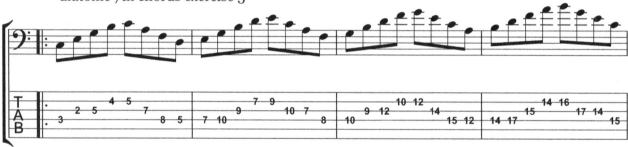

diatonic 7th chords exercise 4

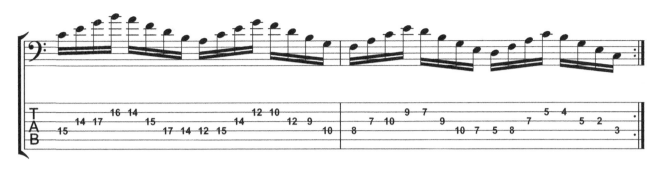

diatonic 7th chords exercise 5

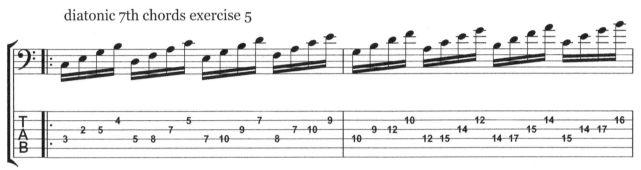

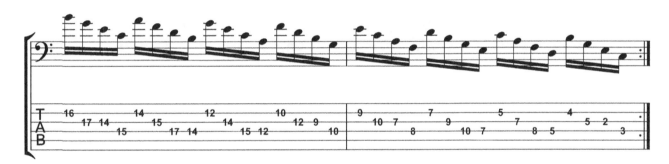

diatonic 7th chords exercise 6

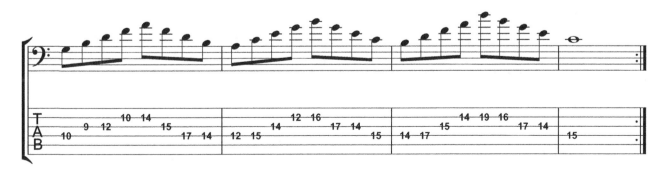

diatonic modes melodic exercise 1 in 2 strings

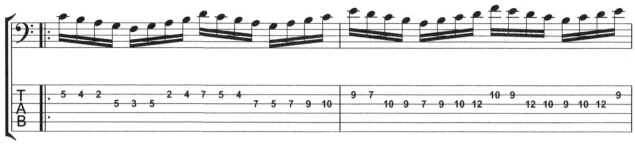

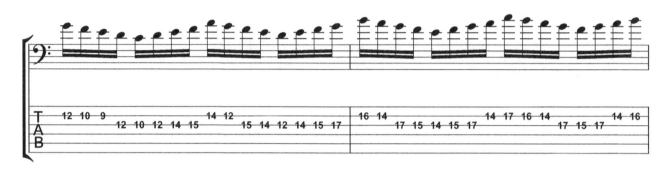

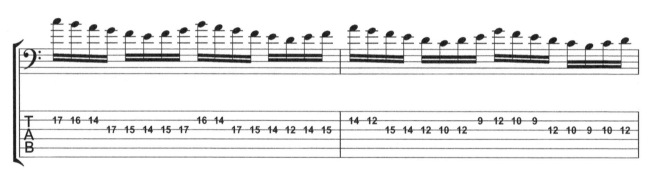

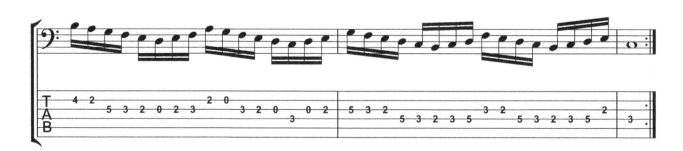

diatonic modes melodic exercise 2 in 2 strings

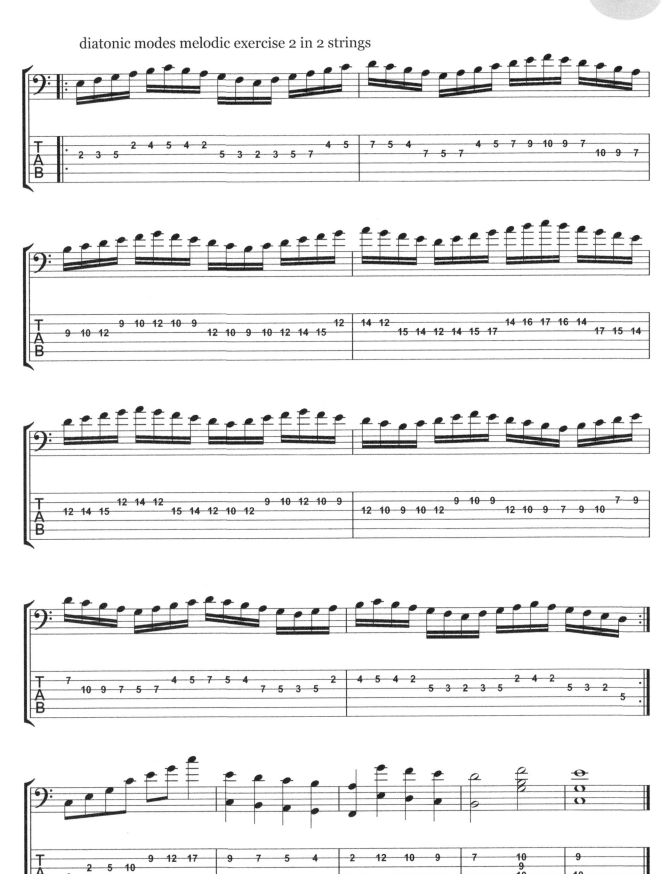

CHAPTER 3

The 5 Positions

The Modes vertically

In this chapter we will examine the vertical positioning of the modes on the fingerboard. This means that we will find in every position, within four or five frets, how many complete modes we can play without moving horizontally on the fingerboard, but moving only vertically on all the strings.

Position 7-1

The first position is position 7-1, which is the position where we find the 7th and 1st modes of a key center on the low string of the 6 string Bass guitar, the B string. For example, if we want to find the first position of the D major key center, we find the note C♯ and next to it the note D, which are respectively the 7th and 1st degrees of the D major tonality. Based on this, we find what other complete mode we can play in the same position, but using only the shape we have learned and no other fingering. From there we see that we are able to play the 7th and the 1st mode with the tonic on the B string, the 3rd and the 4th mode with the tonic on the E string, the 6th mode with tonic on the A string, and the 2nd mode with tonic on the D string.

Position 2

In position 2 we find the 2nd mode with the tonic note on the B string, the 5th mode with the tonic on the E string, the 7th and 1st modes with tonic on the A string, and the 3rd and 4th modes with the tonic on the D string.

Position 3-4

In position 3-4 we find the 3rd and 4th modes with the tonic on the B string, the 6th mode with the tonic on the E string, the 2nd mode with tonic on the A string, and the 5th mode with the tonic on the D string.

Position 5

In position 5 we find the 5th mode with the tonic on the B string, the 7th and 1st modes with the tonic on the E string, the 3rd and 4th modes with tonic on the A string, and the 6th mode with the tonic on the D string.

Position 6

In position 6 we find the 6th mode with the tonic on the B string, the 2nd mode with the tonic on the E string, the 5th mode with tonic on the A string, and the 7th and 1st modes with tonic on the D string.

Secret Scales

In the progression of the exercises and once we recognize for each position the modes that we used for its structure, we will see that we are able to play and many others of the remaining modes but with a different shape and fingering from the one we have learned so far. Those are the **"secret scales and chords"** as I like to call them because even though we have studied them in the exercises that we have already covered for each position, we had not recognized them until now, which will lead us to the complete construction of each position with all the modes and their diatonic chord arpeggios.

Based on the appearance of all the modes and their chords in every position we will see which new fingerings we need to use for each mode.

In position 7-1 we find as secret scales the 2nd mode which starts with the fourth finger at the B string, the 5th mode which starts with the fourth finger on the E string, the 7th mode which starts with the third finger and the 1st mode which starts with the fourth finger, both on the A string.

In position 2 we find as secret scales the 3rd mode which starts with the third finger and the 4th mode which starts with the fourth finger both on the B string, the 6th mode which starts with the fourth finger on the E string, and the 2nd mode wich starts with the fourth finger at the A string.

In position 3-4 we find as secret scales the 5th mode which starts with the fourth finger at the B string, the 7th mode which starts with the third finger and the 1st mode which starts with the fourth finger both at the E string, and the 3rd mode wich starts with the third finger and 4th mode wich starts with the forth finger both on the A string.

In position 5 we find as secret scales the 6th mode which starts with the fourth finger at the B string, the 2nd mode which starts with the fourth finger on the E string, and the 5th mode wich starts with the forth finger on the A string.

In position 6 we find as secret scales the 7th mode which starts with the third finger and the 1st mode which starts with the fourth finger both on the B string, the 3rd mode which starts with the third finger and the 4th mode which starts with the fourth finger both on the E string, and the 6th mode which starts with the fourth finger on the A string.

Progression of the exercises

1. The main modes that form each position, ascending and descending.
2. The 7th chord arpeggios of the main modes, ascending and descending.
3. All the notes of the position as one scale.
4. The notes of the position with broken thirds.
5. The notes of the position with triad arpeggios.
6. All the modes found in each position with secret modes.
7. All the diatonic 7th chords with secret chords arpeggio.
8. Practice of the entire position with sets of four sixteenth notes.
9. The triads and 7th chords with arpeggios of the main mode(s) where each position starts.
10. Diatonic voice harmony

Position 7-1 studies
VII- I
III-IV
VI
II

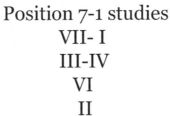

main modes

main chords

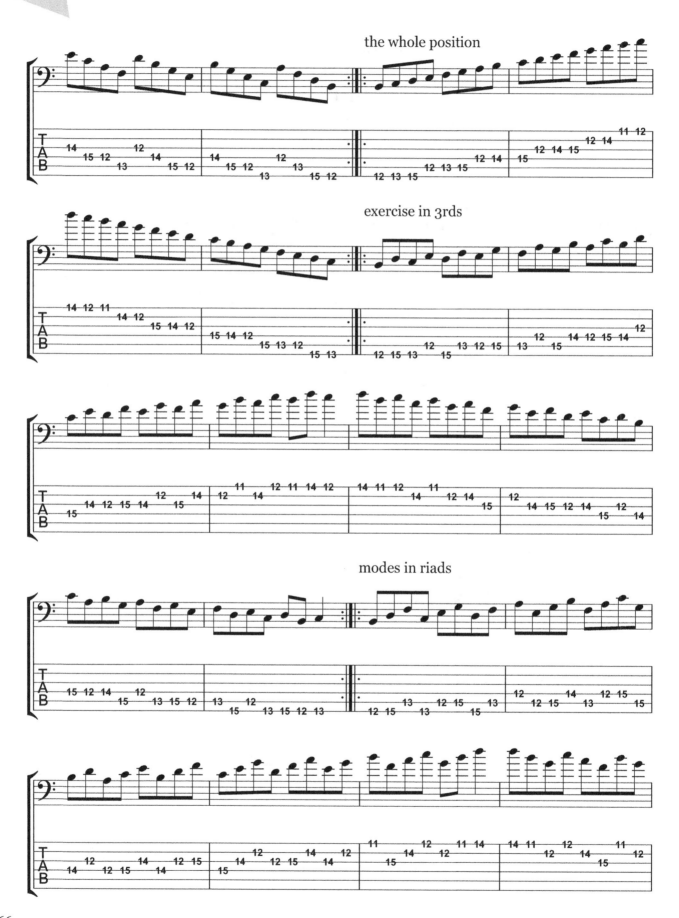

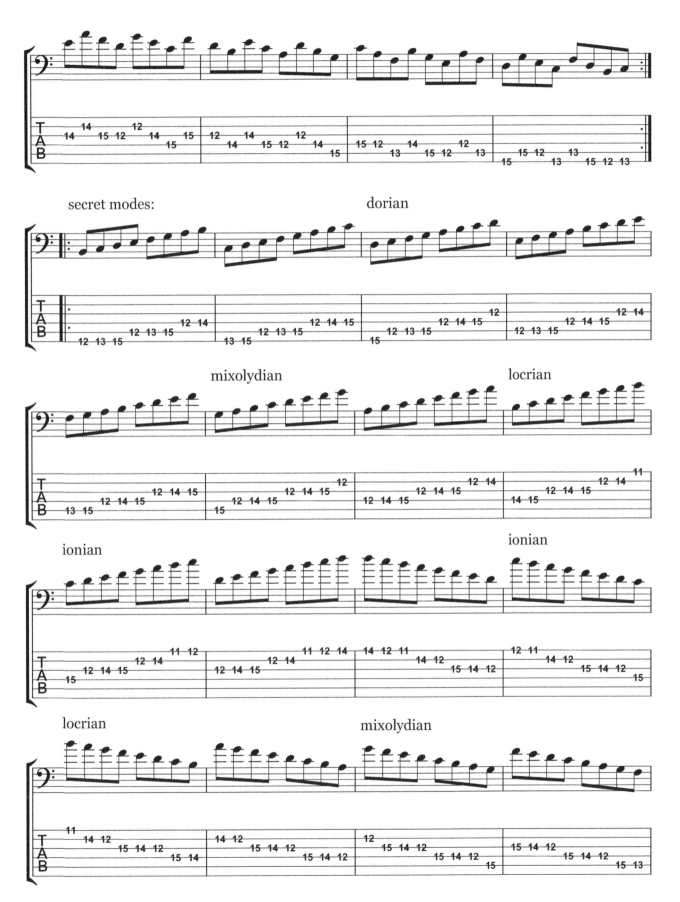

secret modes:

dorian

mixolydian

locrian

ionian

ionian

locrian

mixolydian

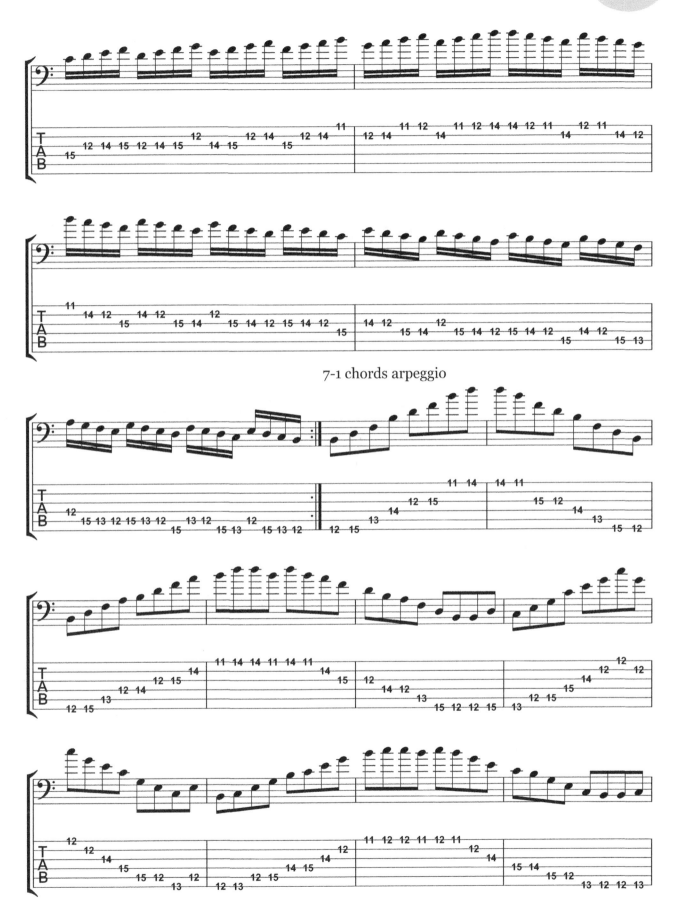

7-1 chords arpeggio

Position 2 studies
II
V
VII-I
III-IV

main modes

main chords

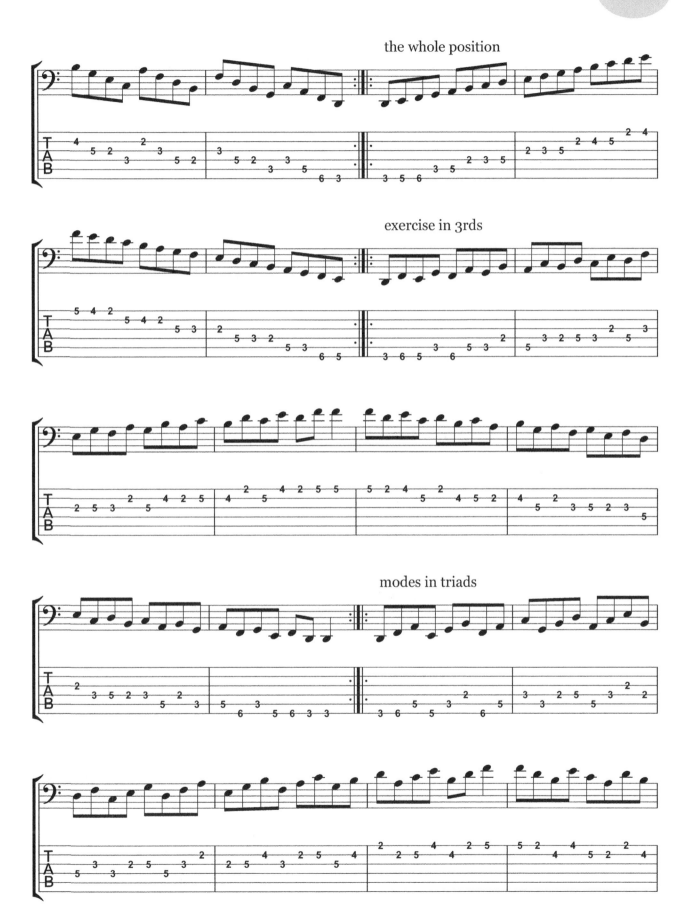

the whole position

exercise in 3rds

modes in triads

secret modes: phrygian   lydian

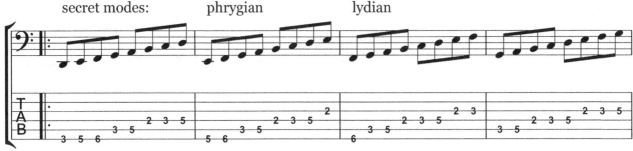

aeolian   dorian

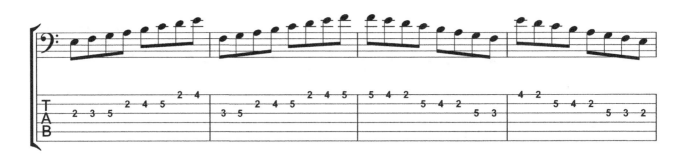

dorian   aeolian

2 chord arpeggio

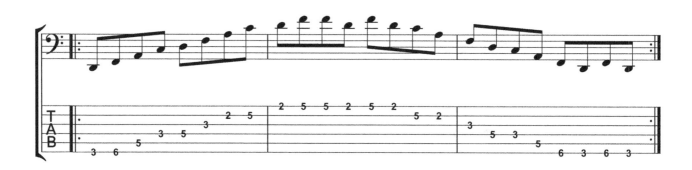

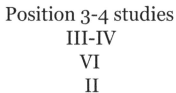

Position 3-4 studies
III-IV
VI
II
V

main modes

main chords

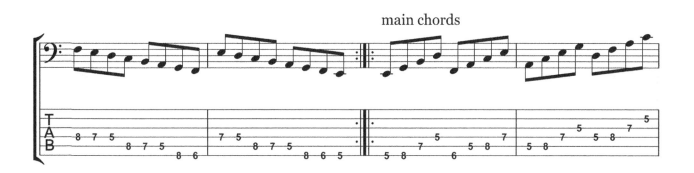

the whole position

exercise in 3rds

modes in triads

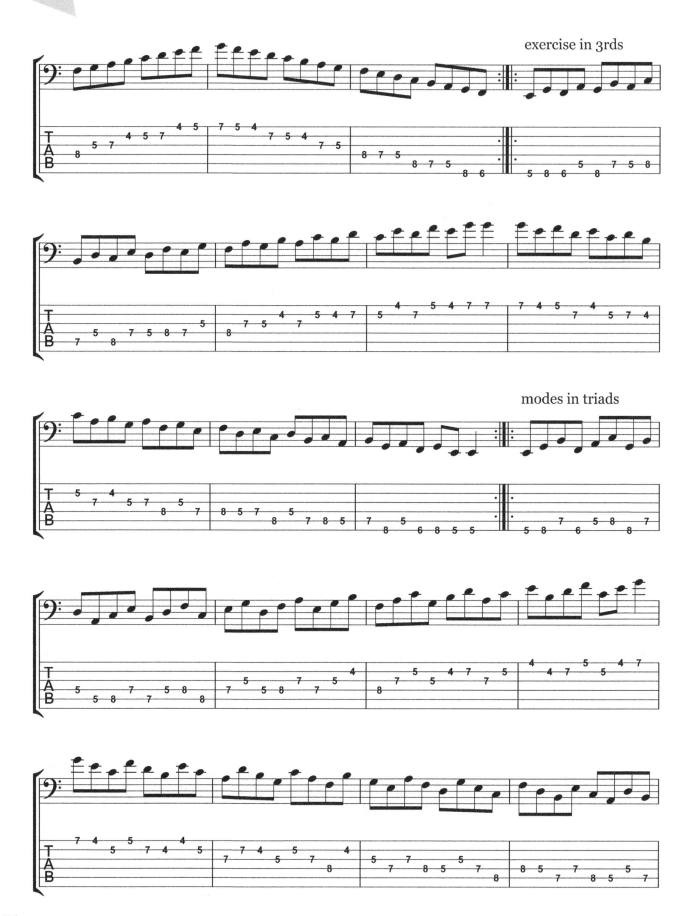

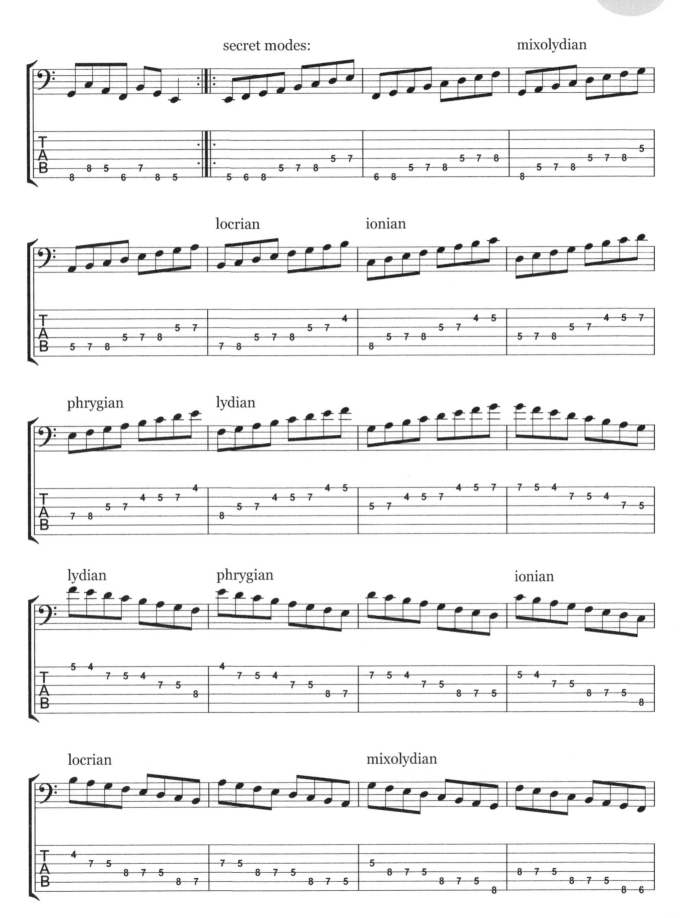

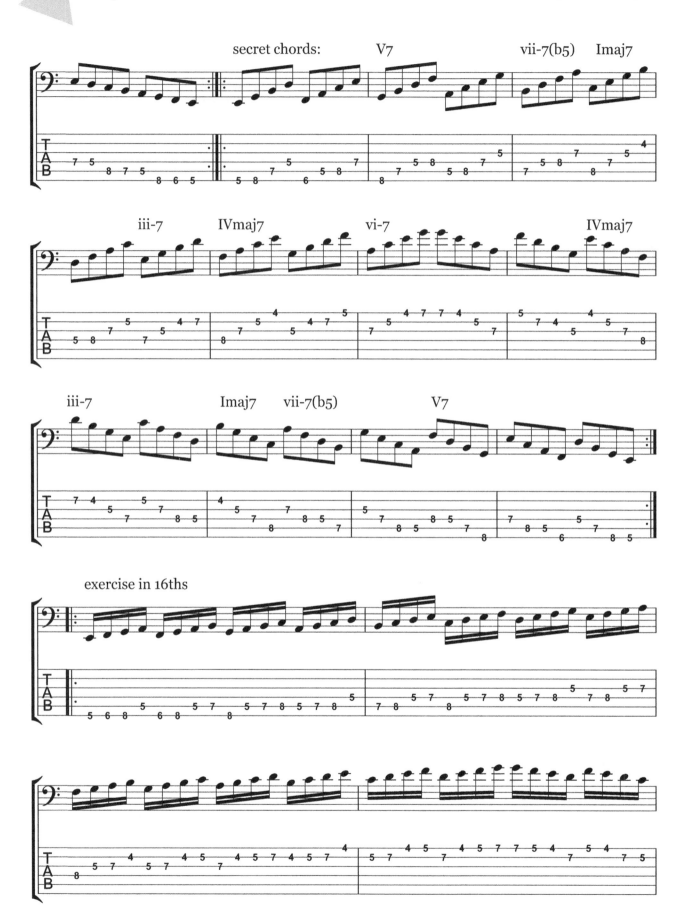

3-4 chord arpeggios

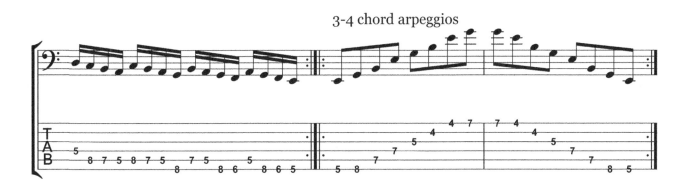

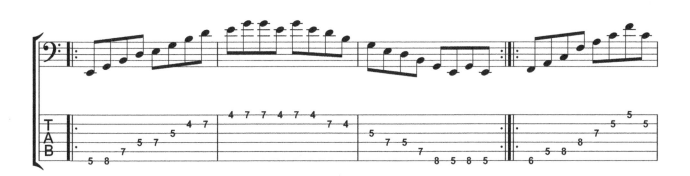

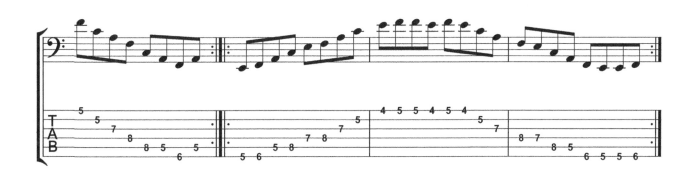

Position 5 studies
V
VII-I
III-IV
VI

main modes

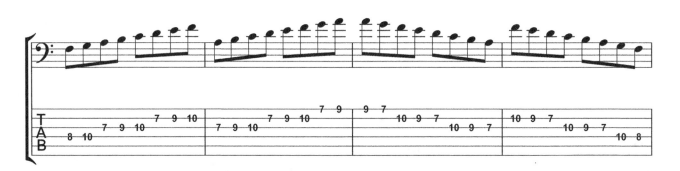

main chords

the whole position

exercise in 3rds

modes in triads

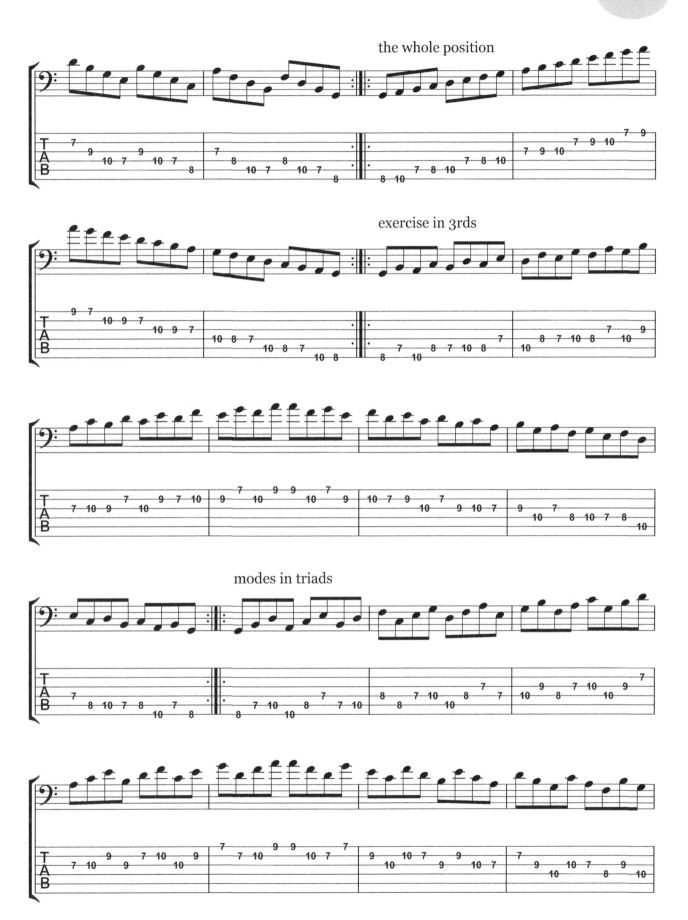

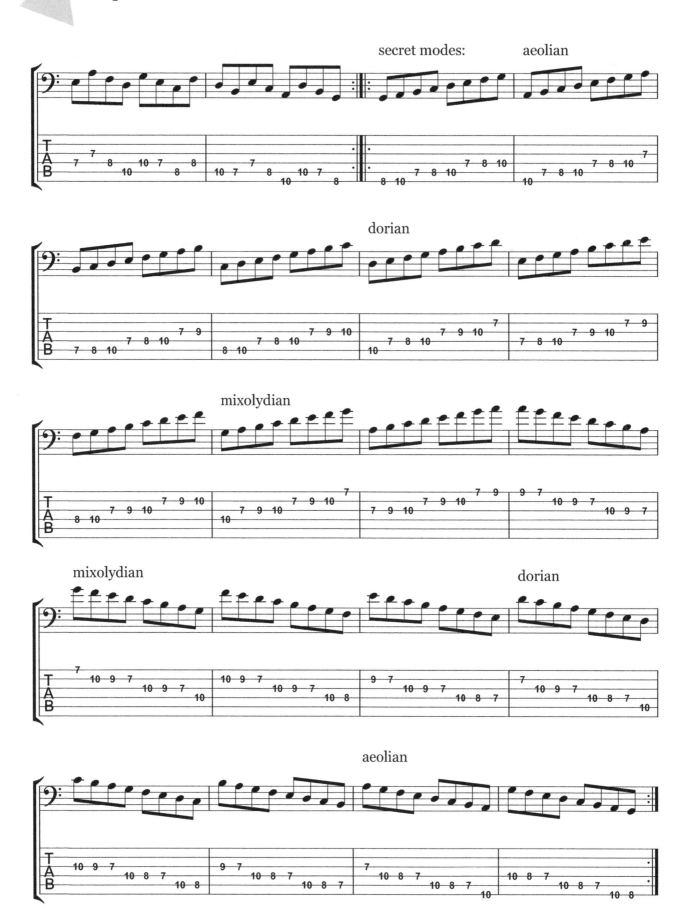

5 chord arpeggios

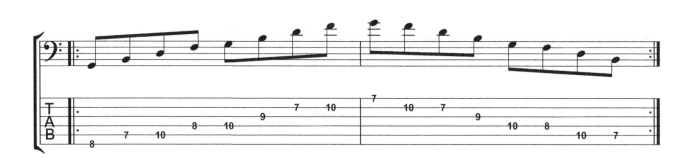

Position 6 studies
VI
II
V
VII-I

main modes

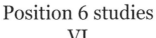

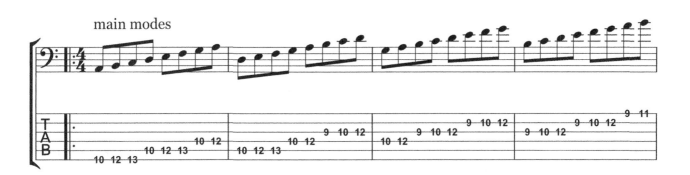

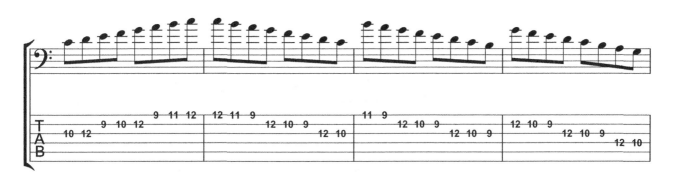

main chords

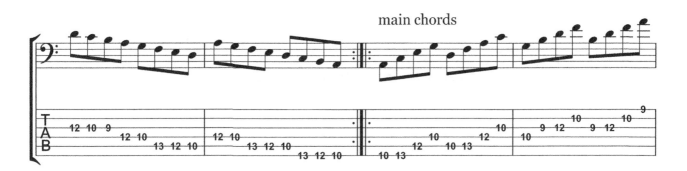

the whole position

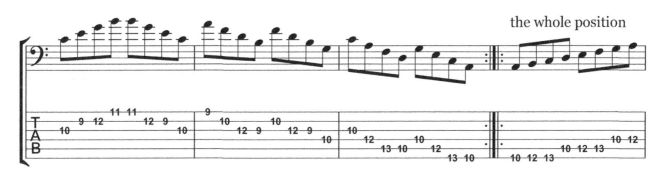

exercise in 3rds

modes in triads

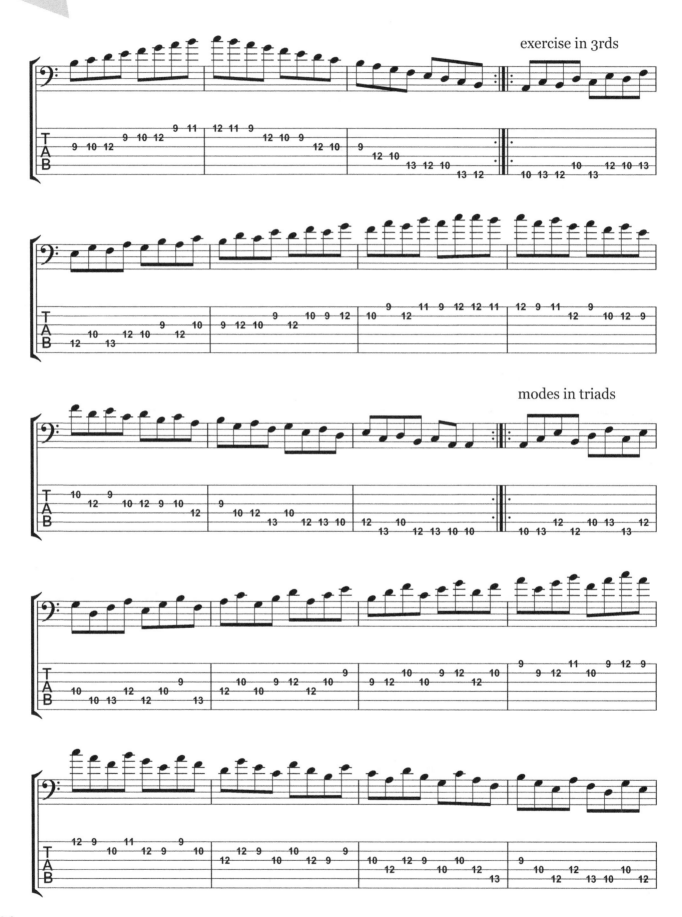

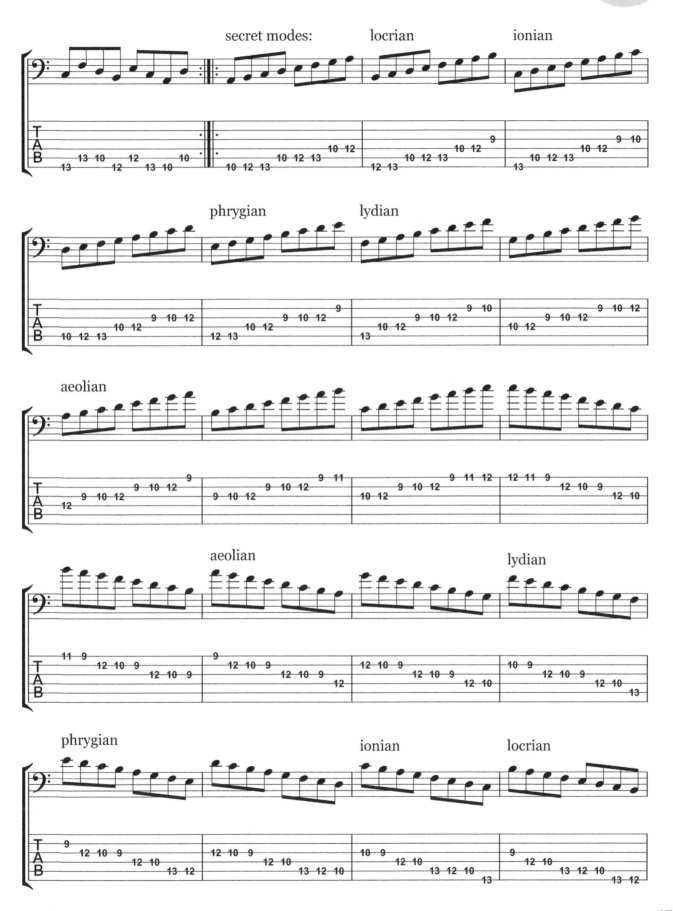

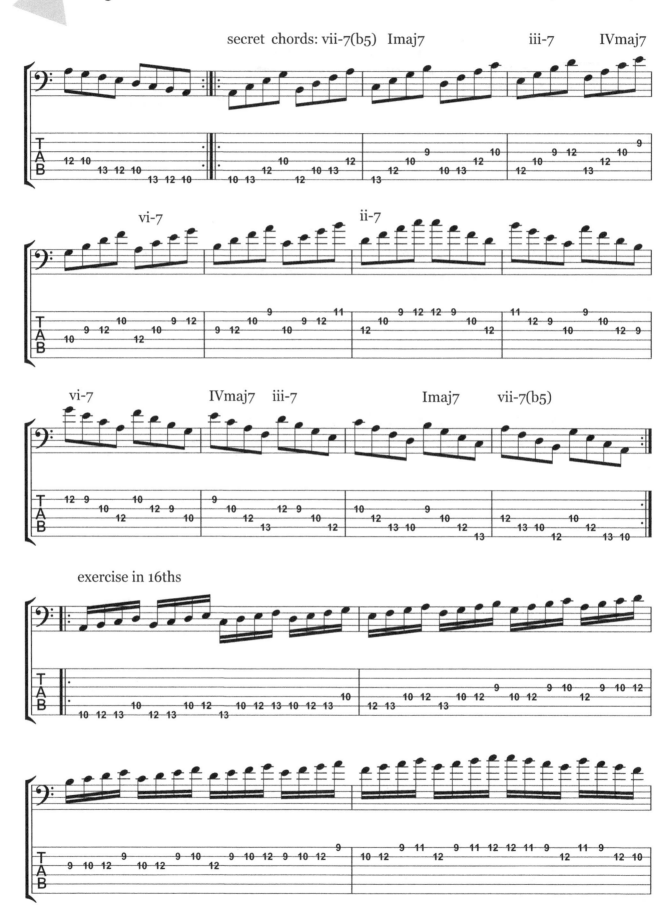

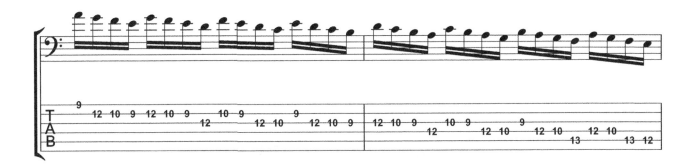

6 chord arpeggios

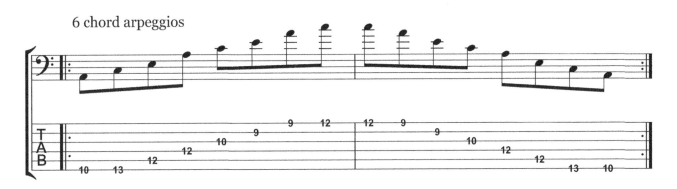

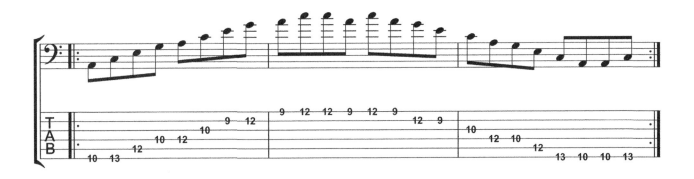

CHAPTER 4

Construction of the diatonic arpeggios in 5 positions

In this chapter we will study in each position the complete construction of the triads and 7th chords along with all their inversions in all seven diatonic scale degrees of the key center. We will do that with the vertical form of each one of the 5 positions with arpeggios. This covers and analyzes their complete placement along each position, which makes this chapter one of the most important ones in this book.

Position 7-1 arpeggio studies

VII/C major key

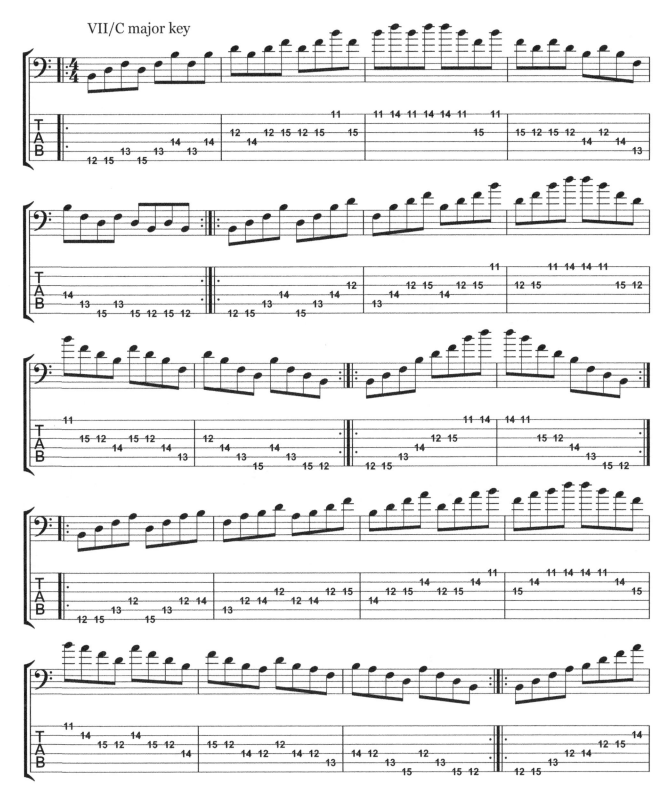

I/C major key

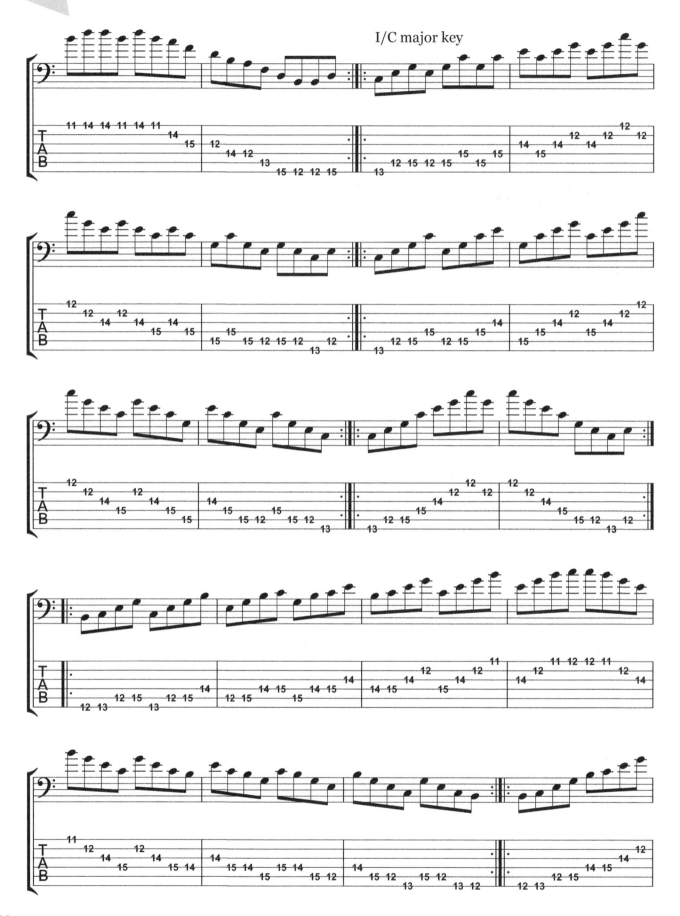

II/C major key

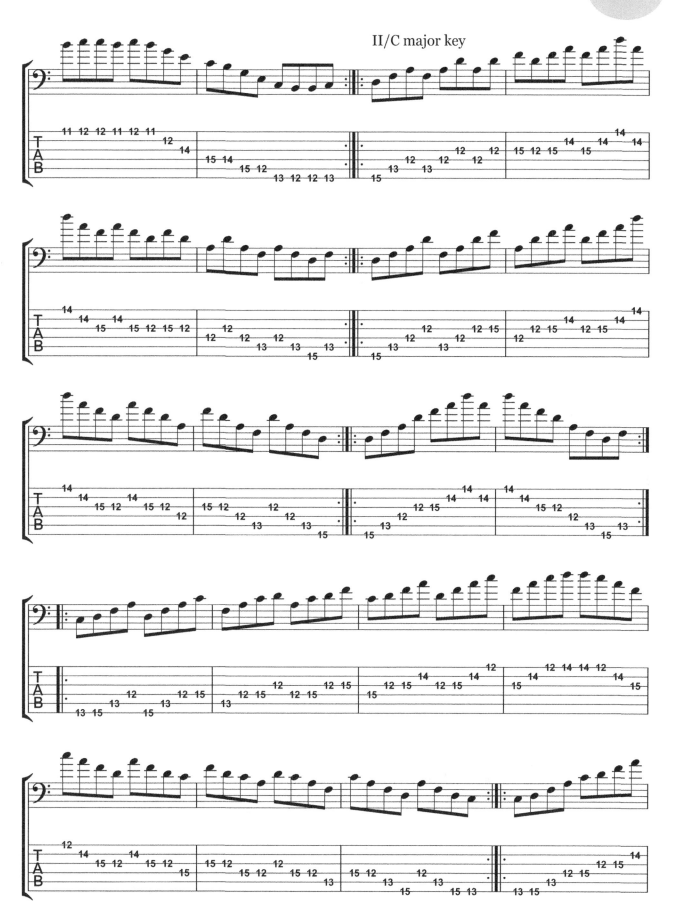

III/C major key

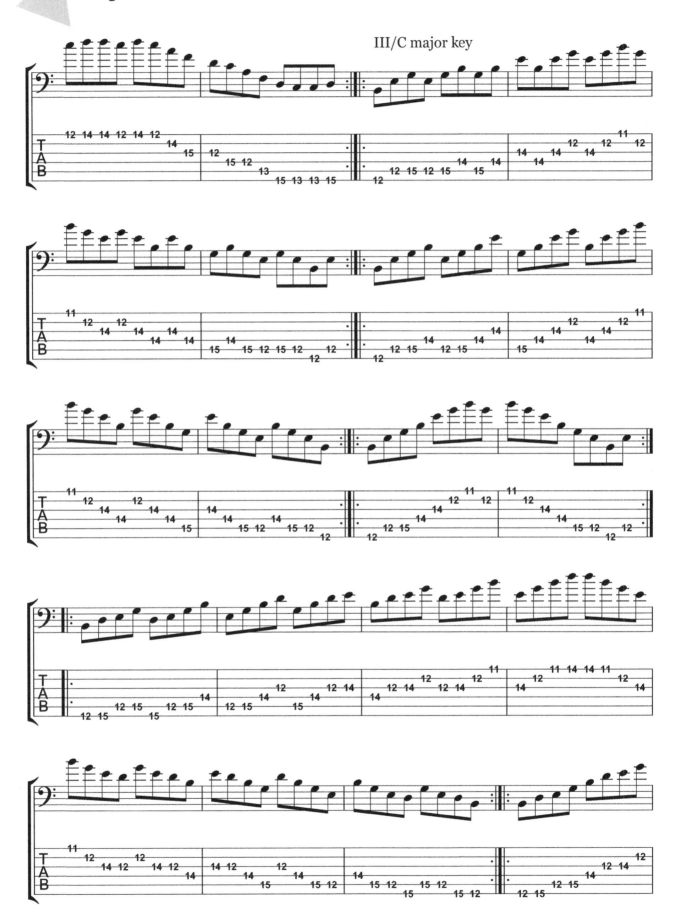

IV/C major key

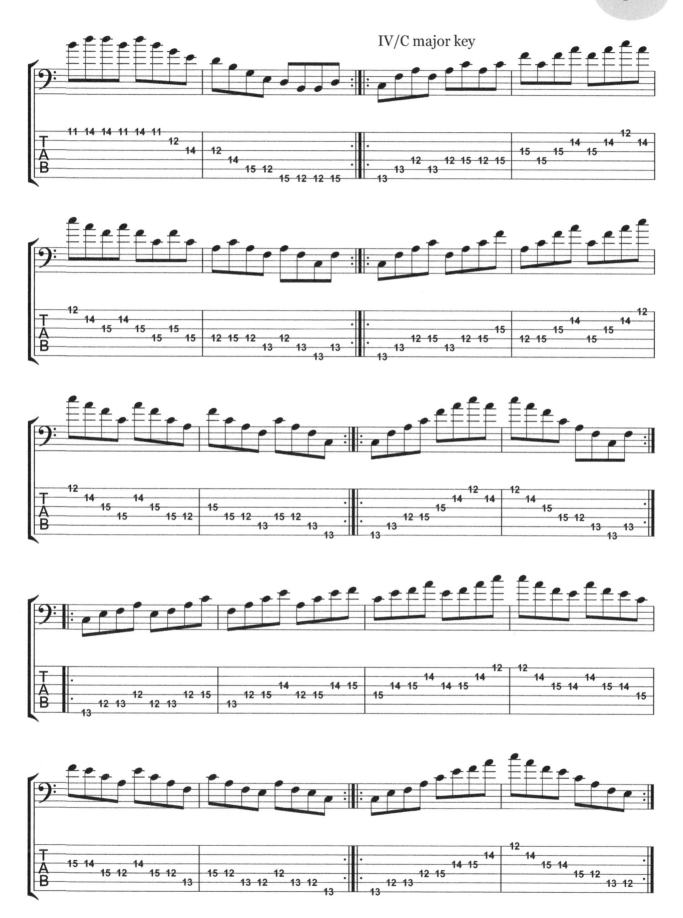

V/C major key

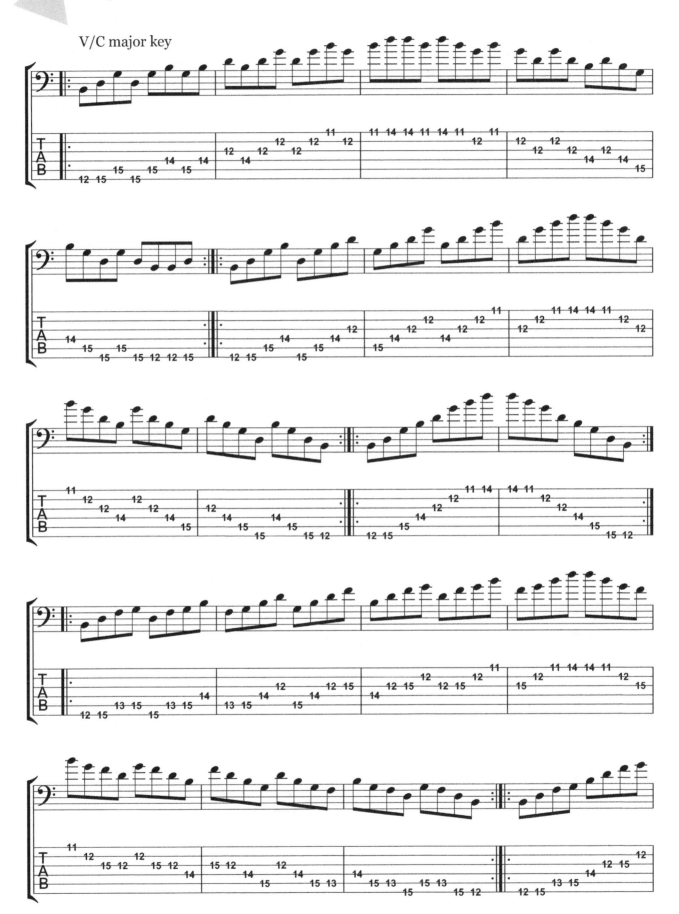

VI/C major key

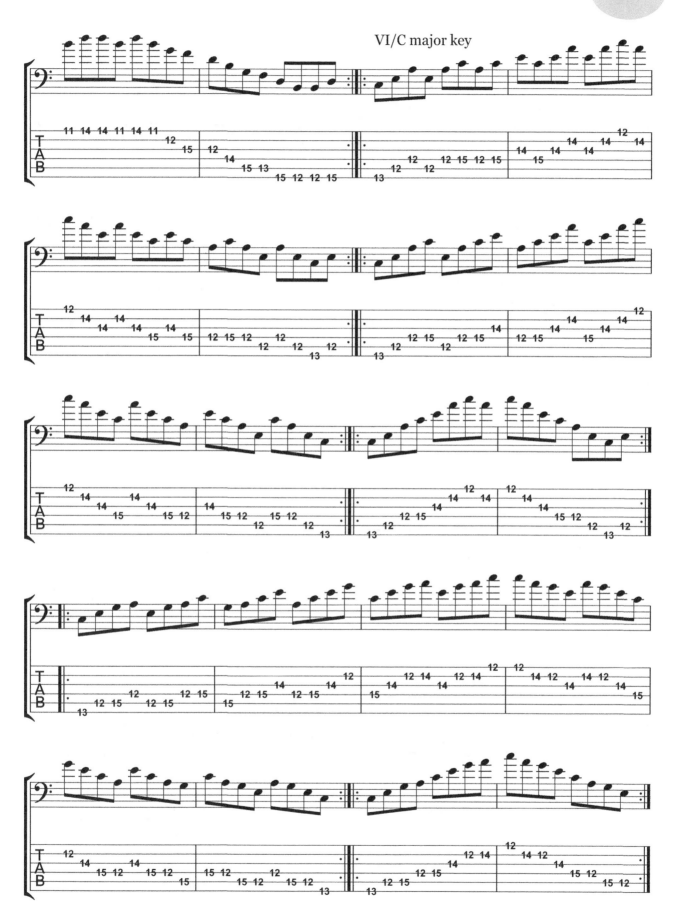

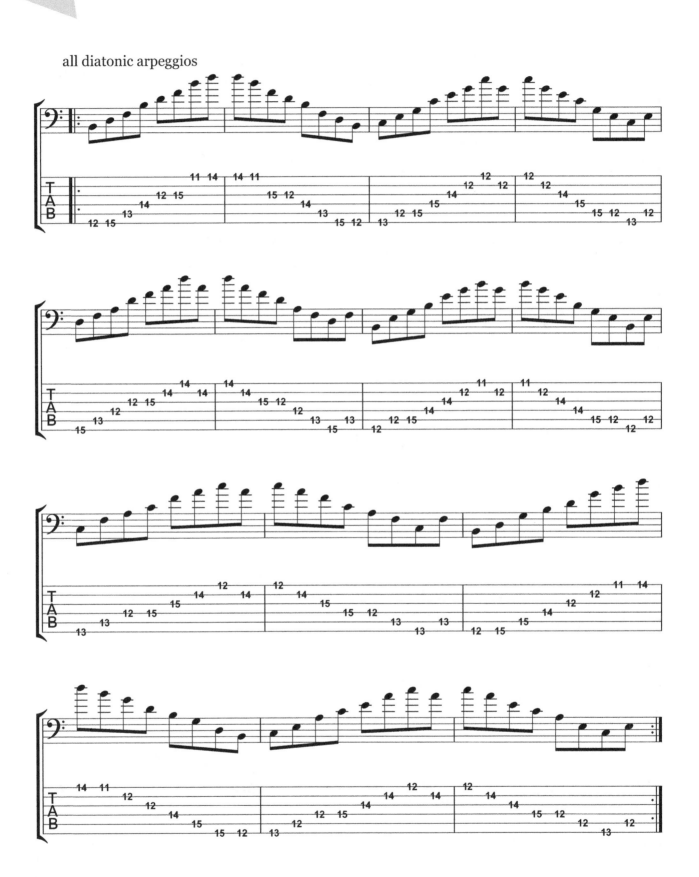

all diatonic arpeggios

Position 2 arpeggio studies

II/C major key

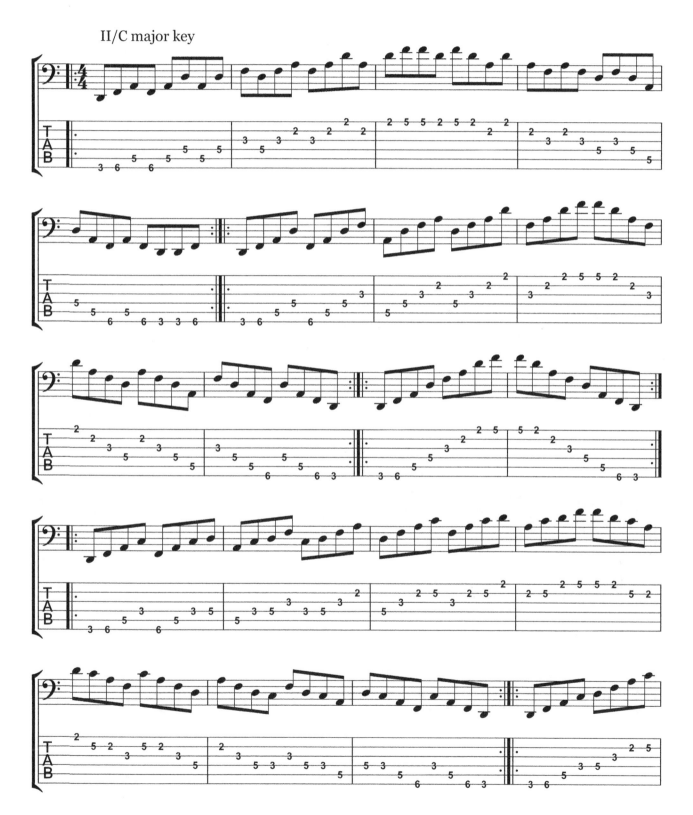

III/C major key

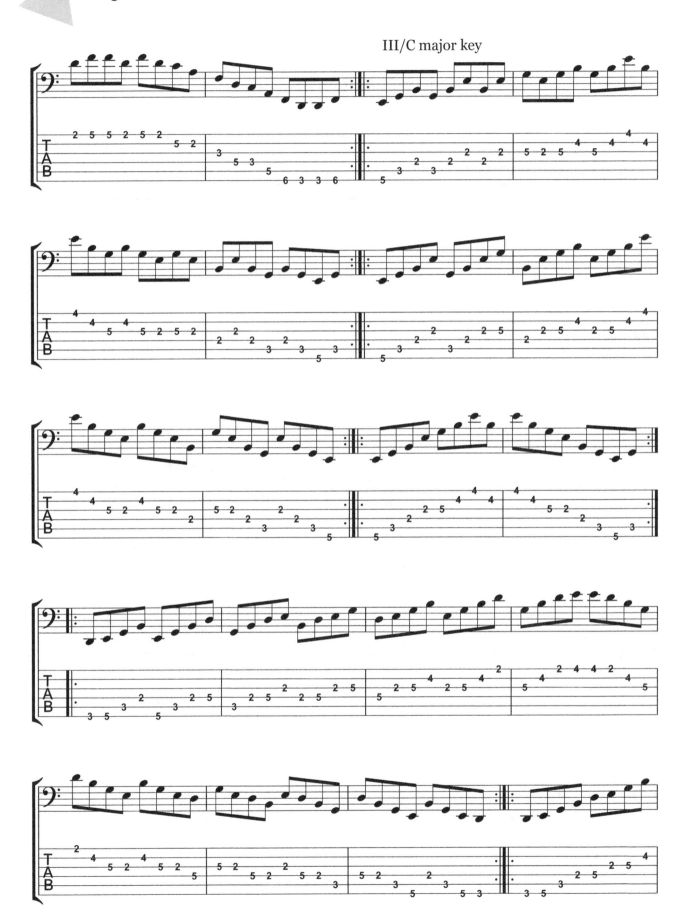

IV/C major key

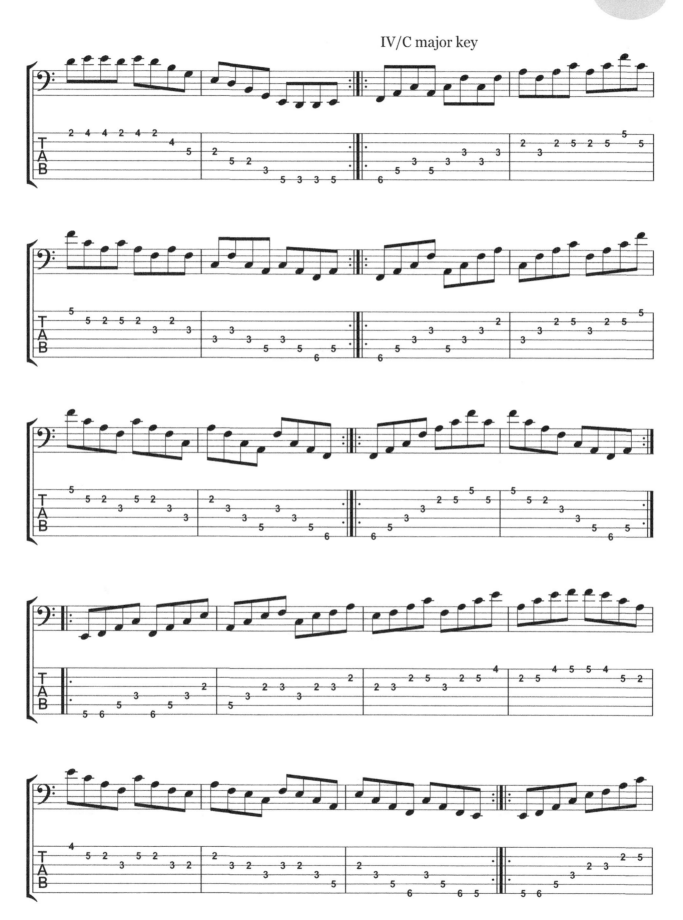

V/C major key

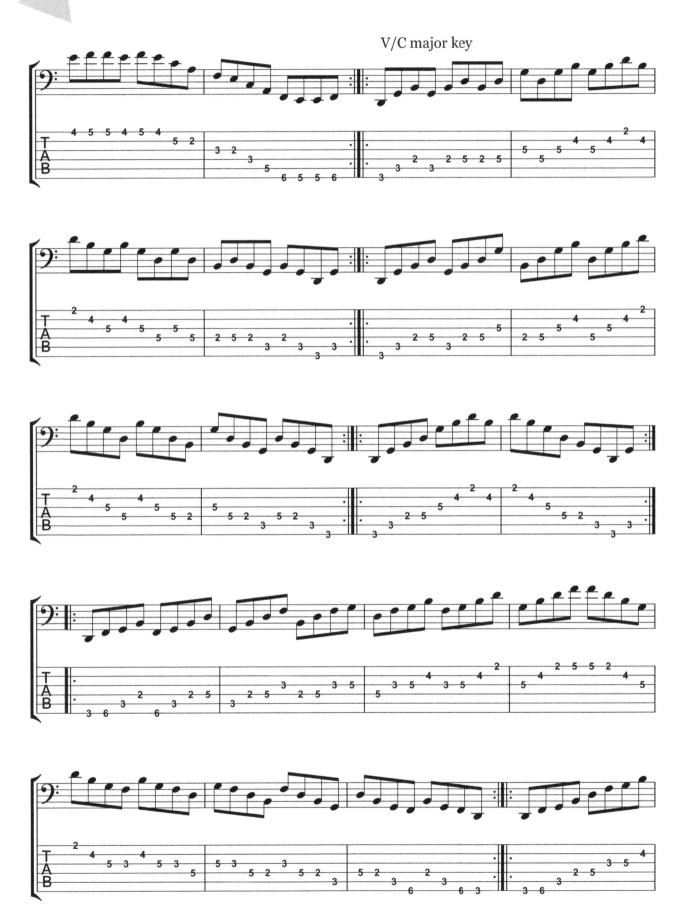

VI/C major key

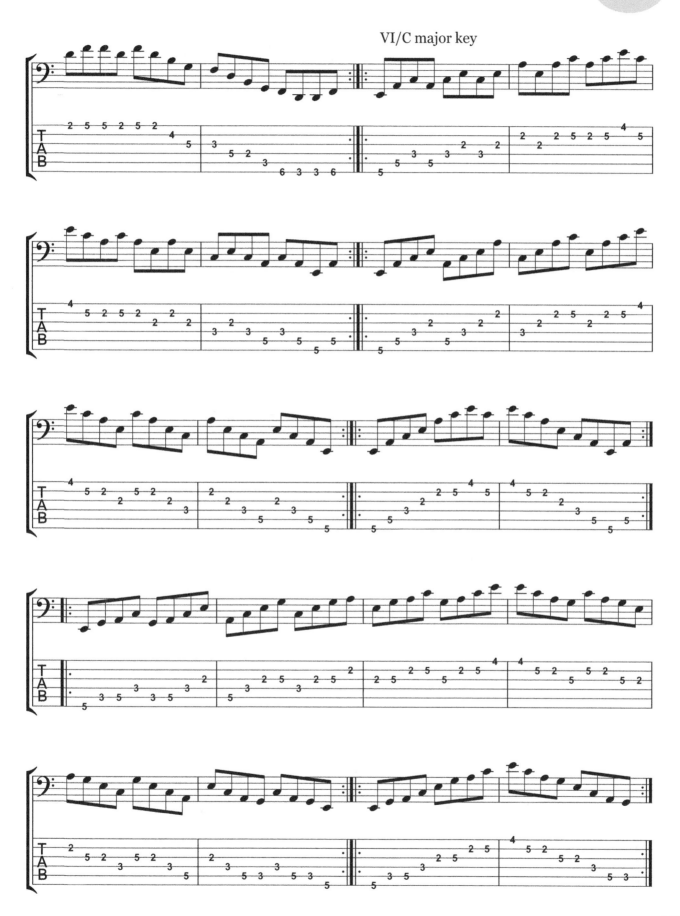

VII/C major key

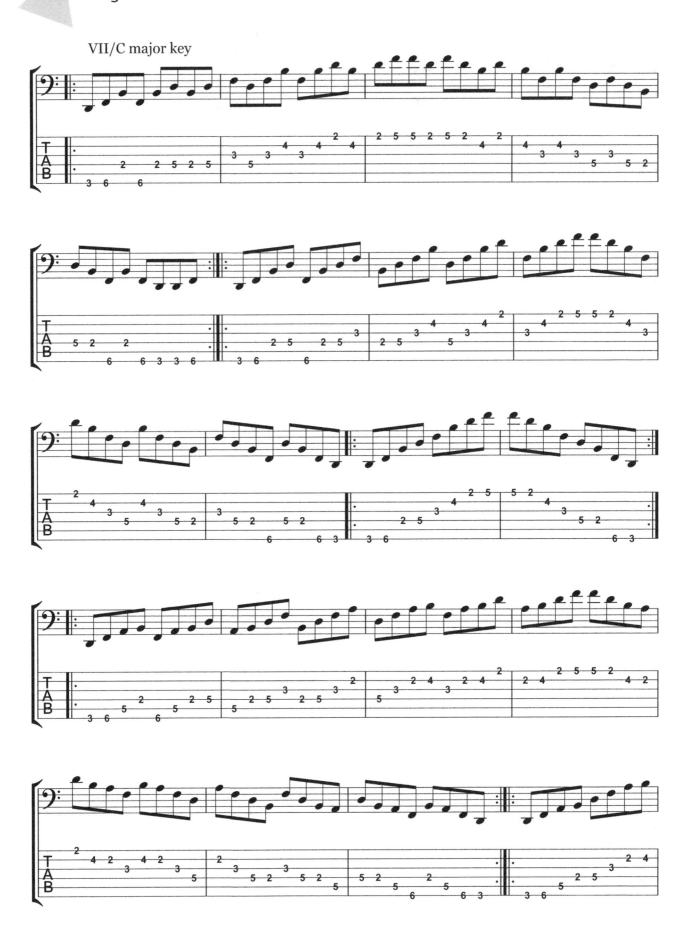

I/C major key

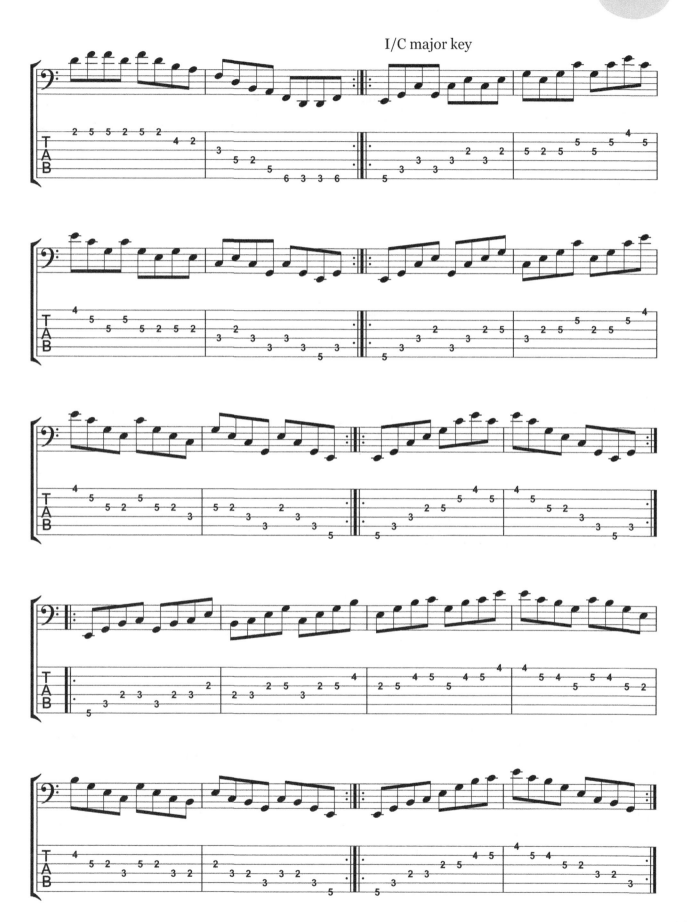

all diatonic arpeggios

Position 3-4 arpeggio studies

III/C major key

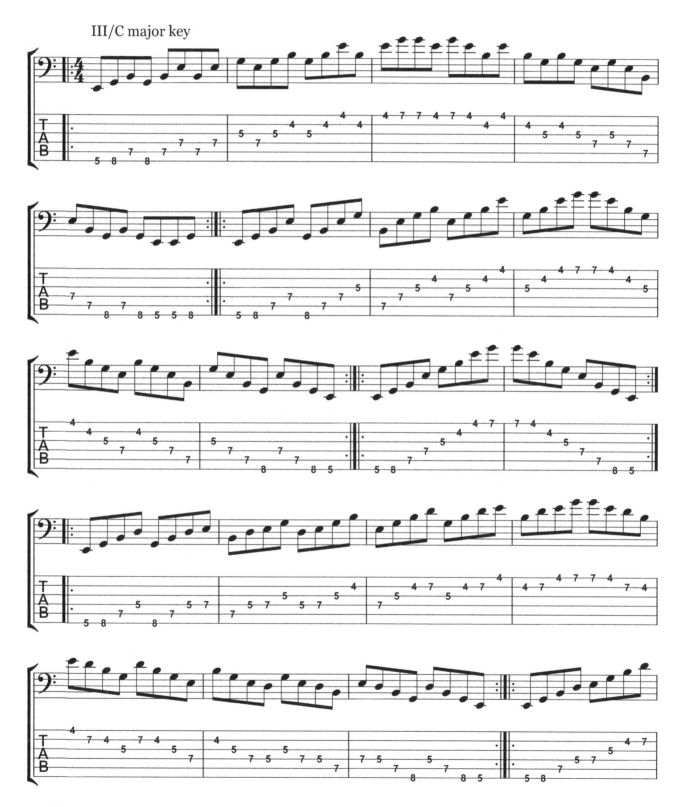

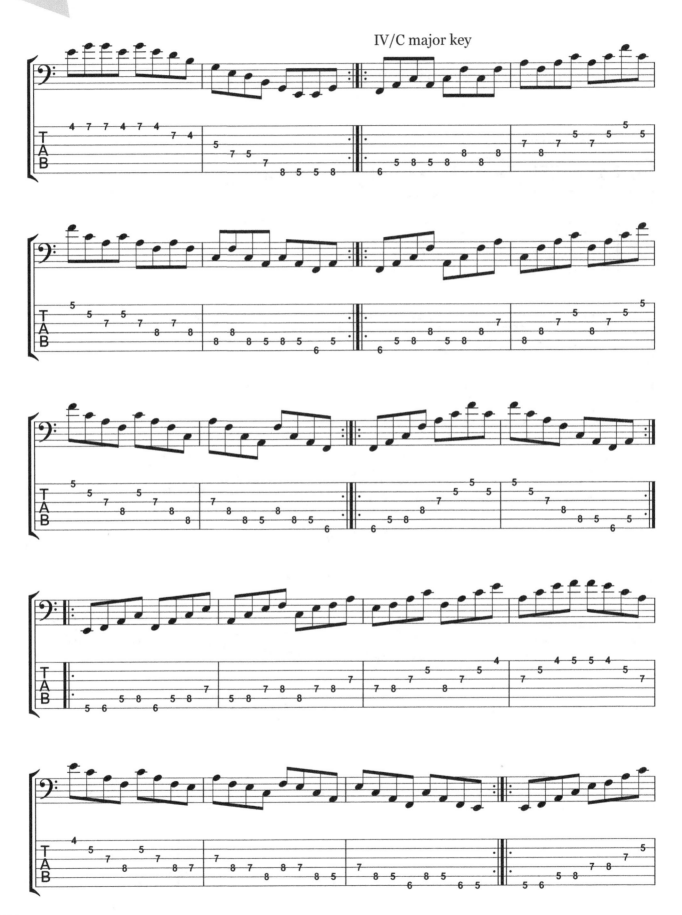

IV/C major key

V/C major key

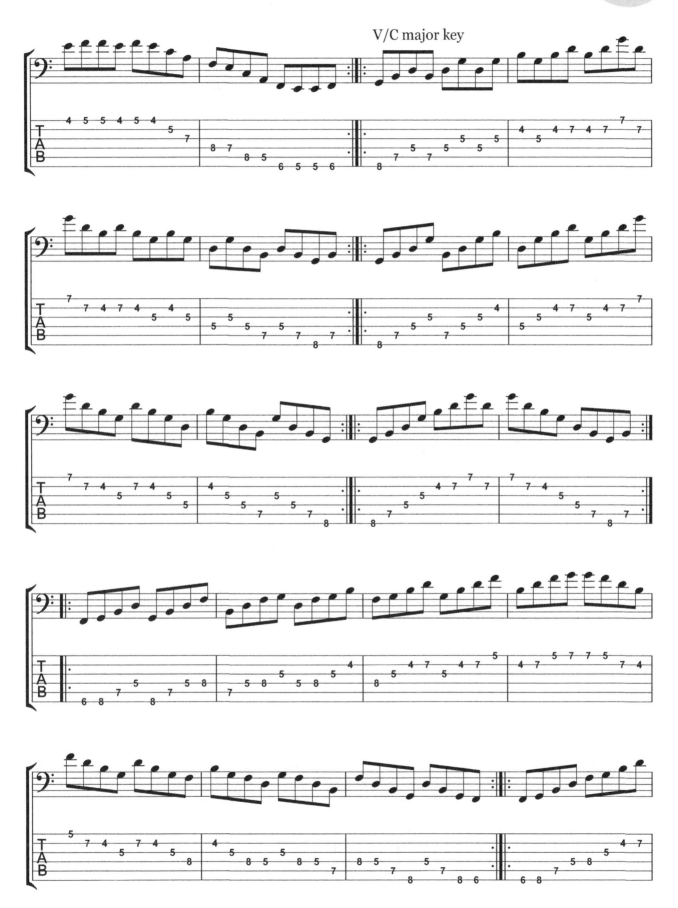

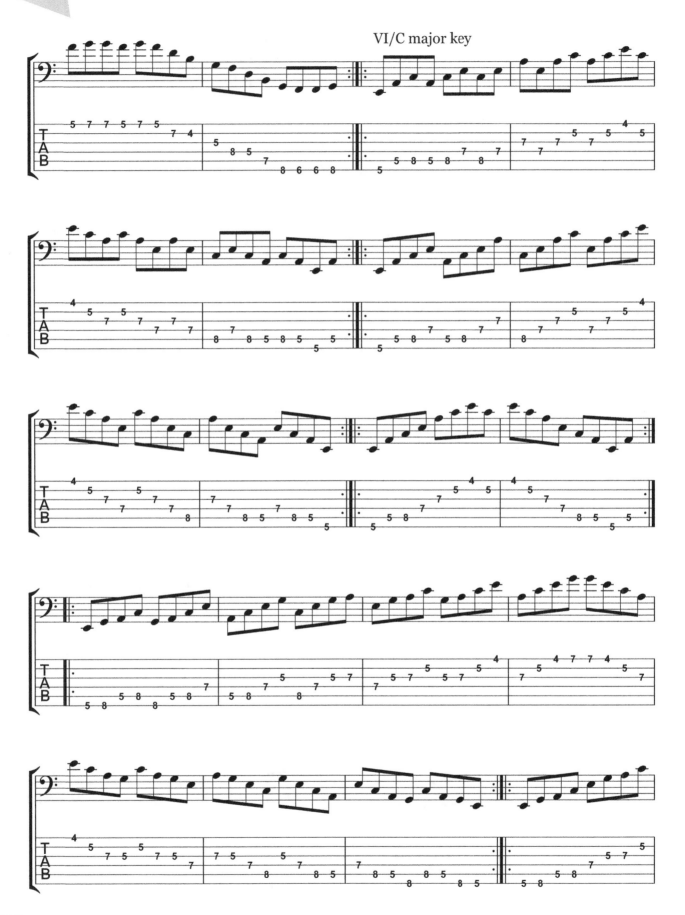

VI/C major key

VII/C major key

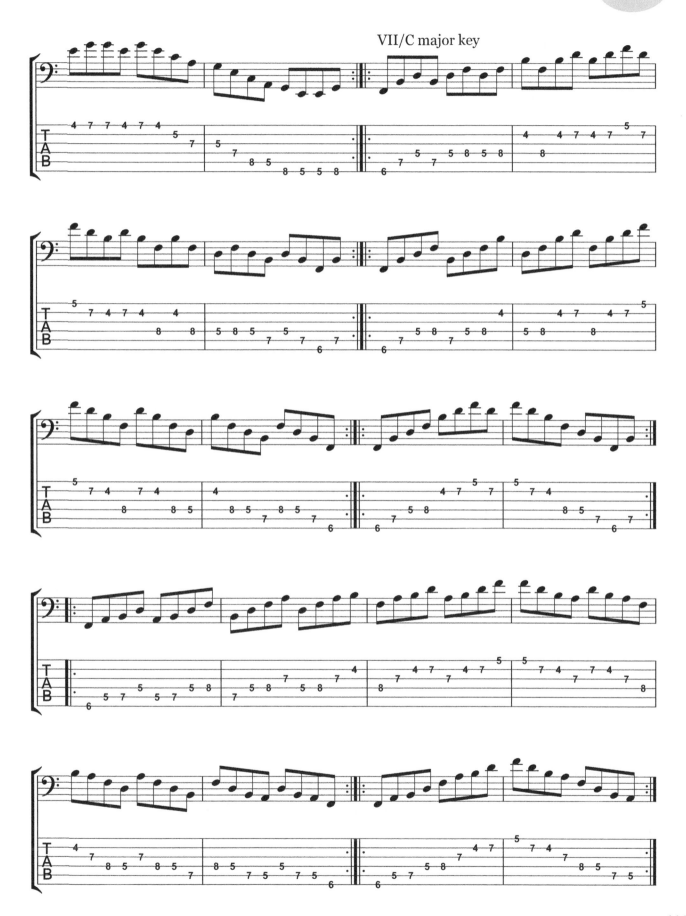

I/C major key

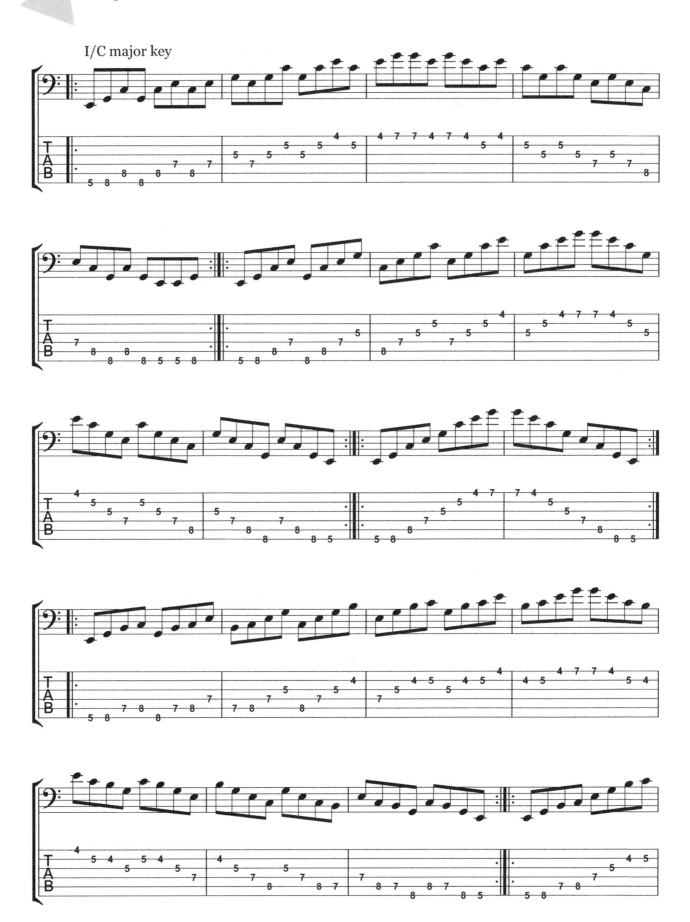

II/C major key

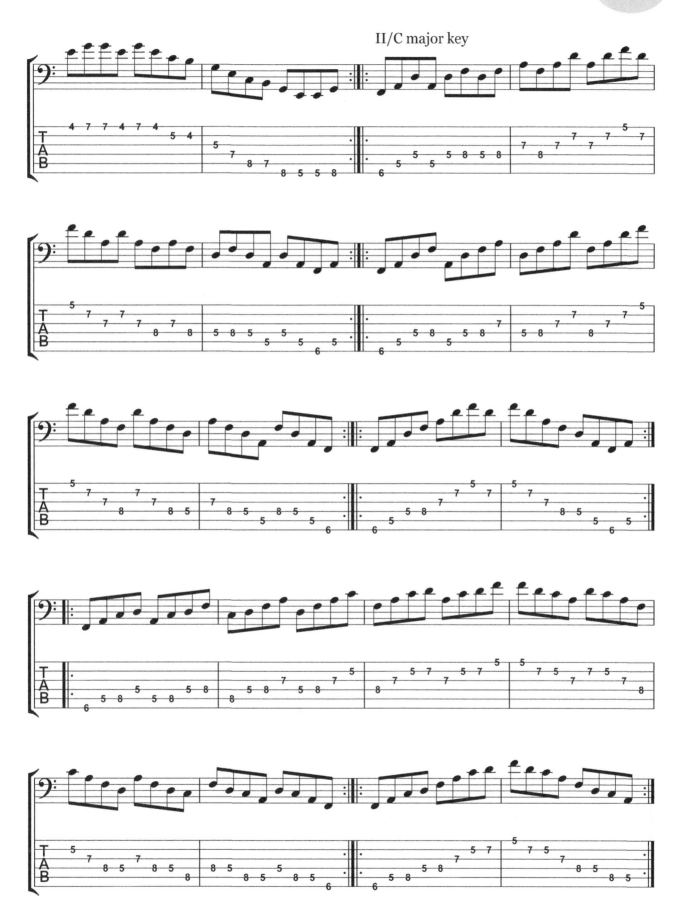

all diatonic arpeggios

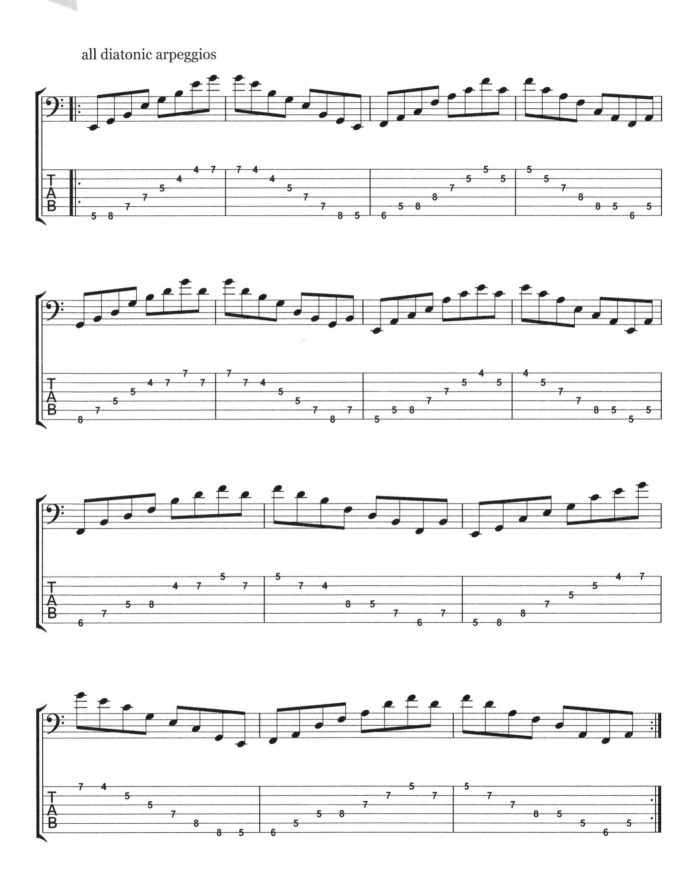

Position 5 arpeggio studies

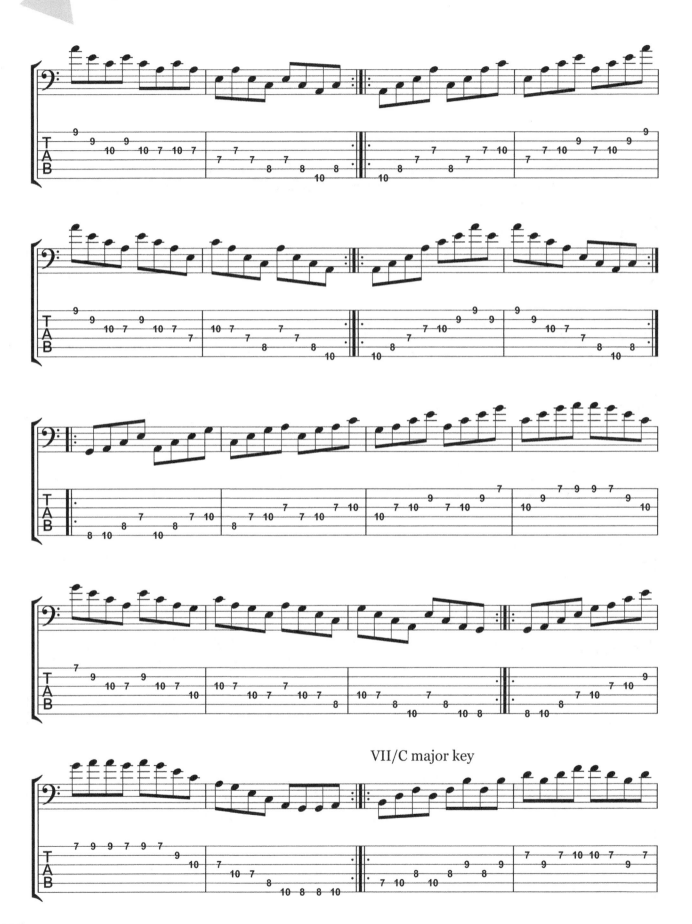

VII/C major key

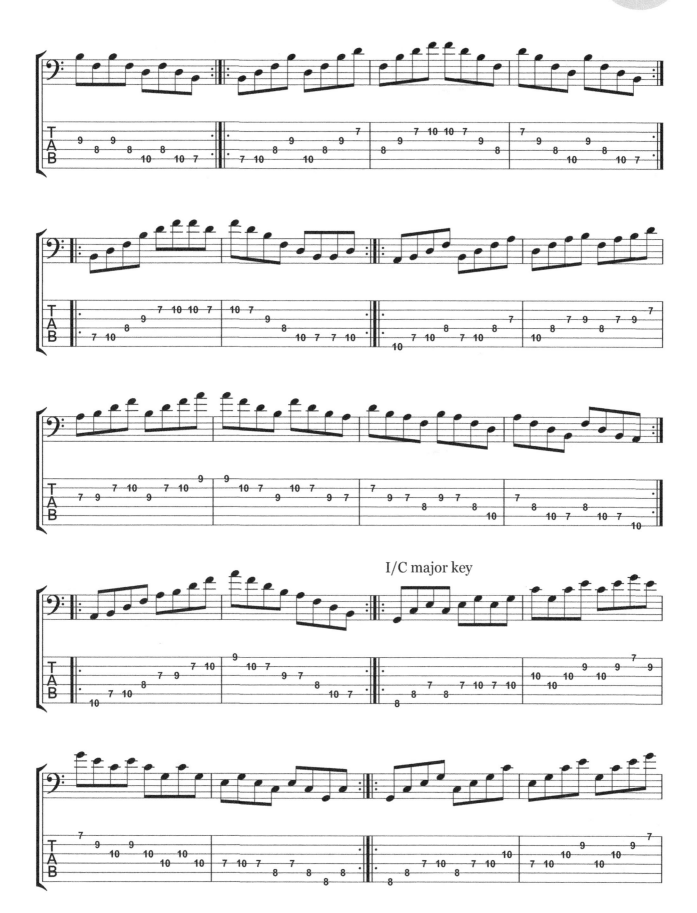

I/C major key

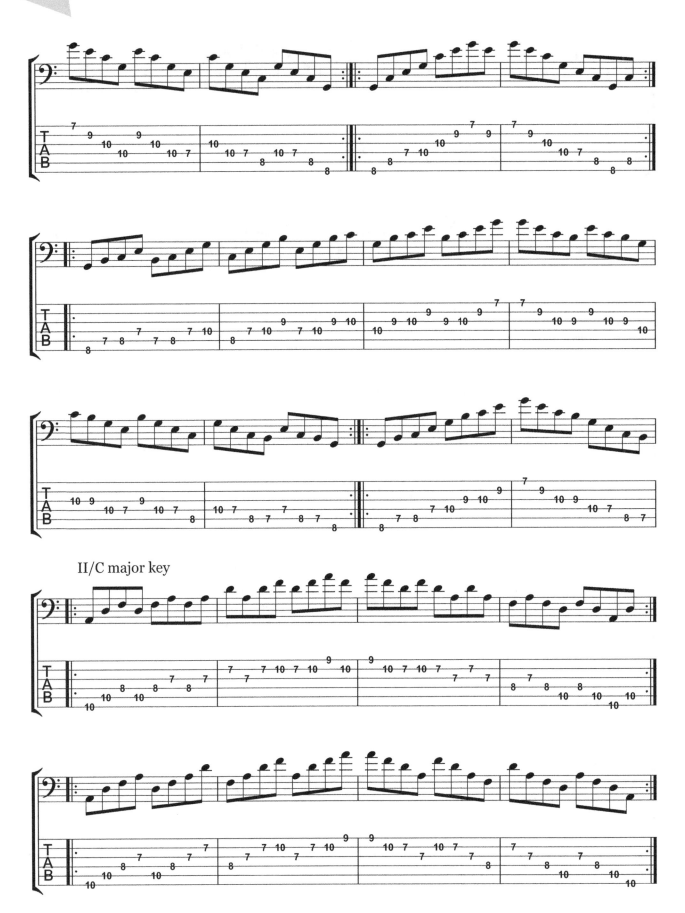

II/C major key

III/C major key

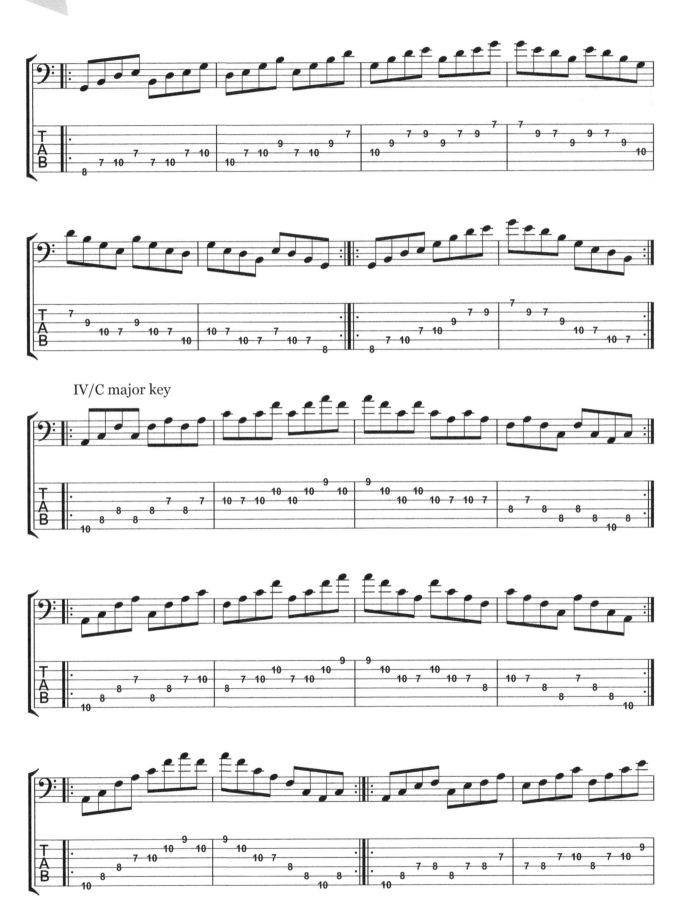

IV/C major key

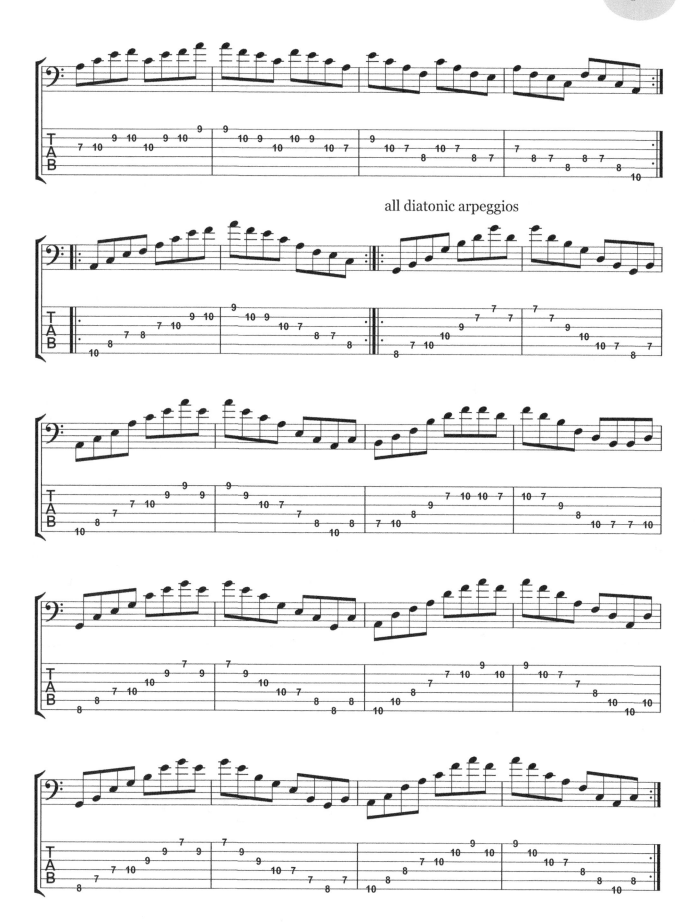

all diatonic arpeggios

Position 6 arpeggio studies

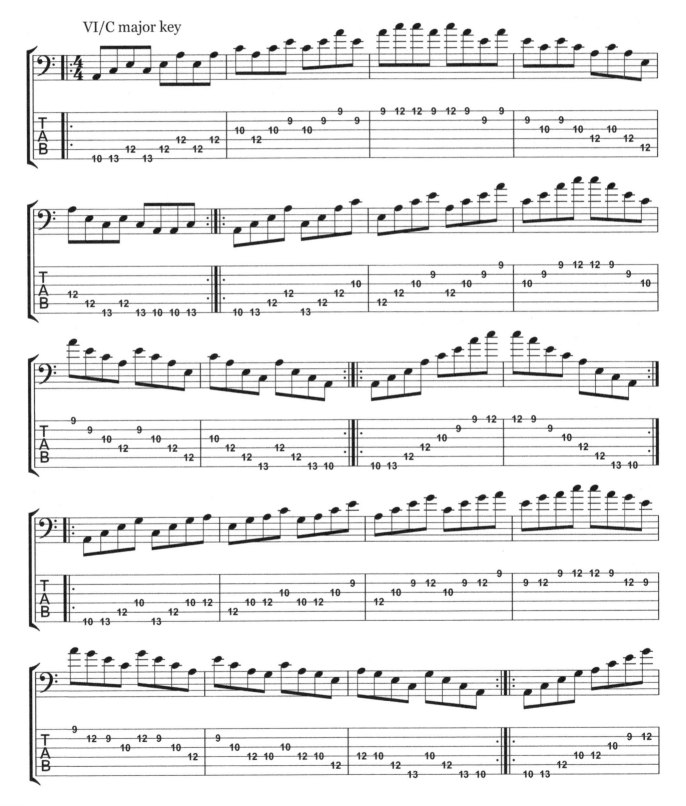

VII/C major key

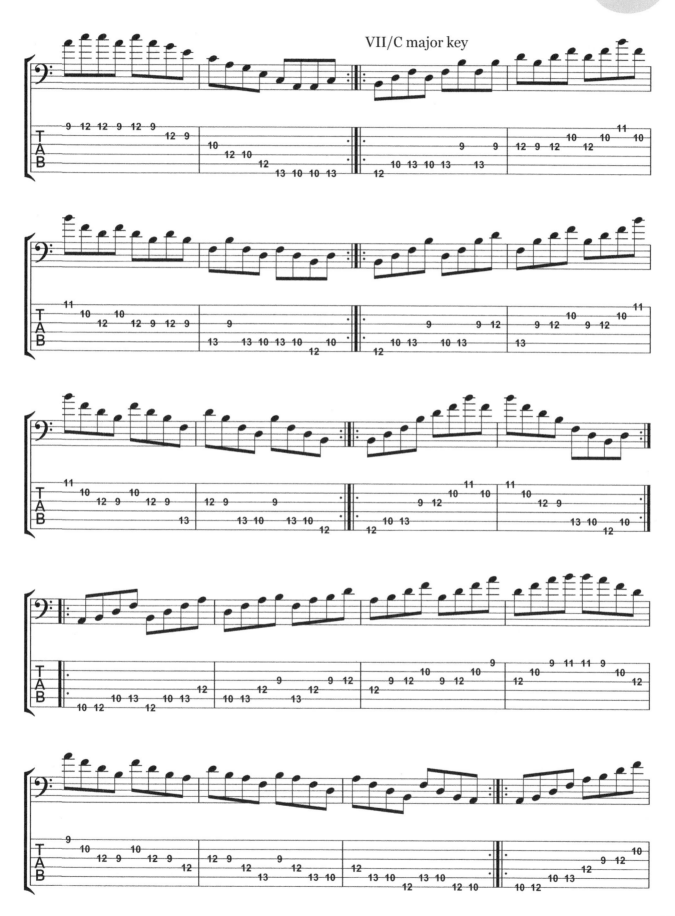

I/C major key

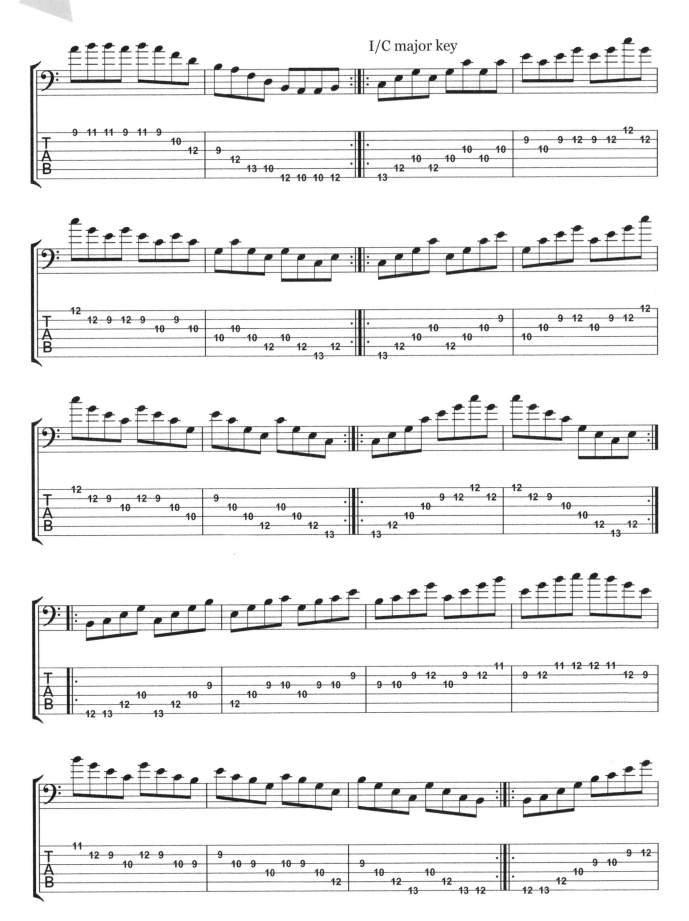

II/C major key

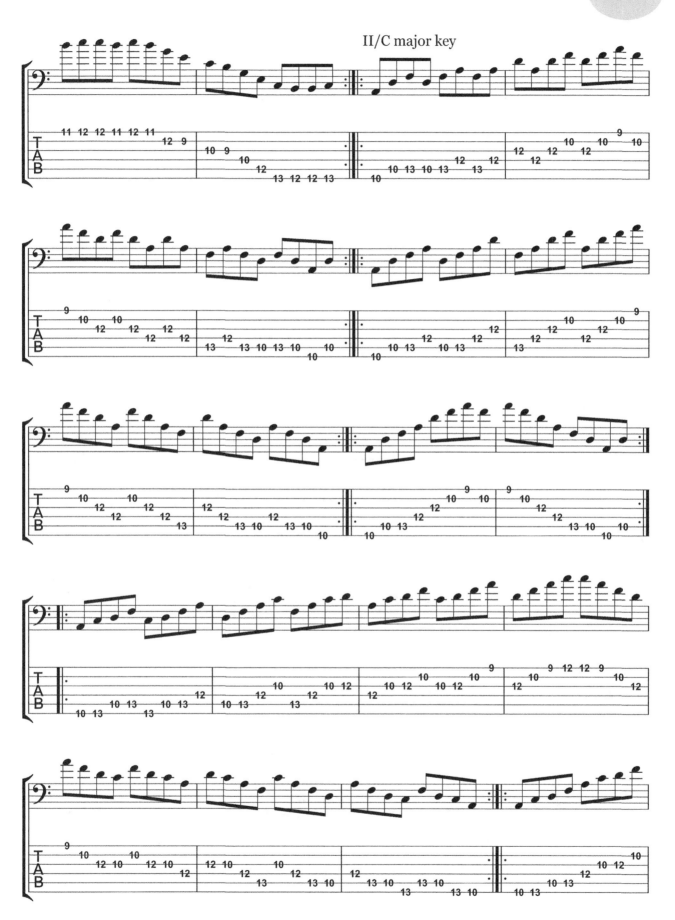

III/C major key

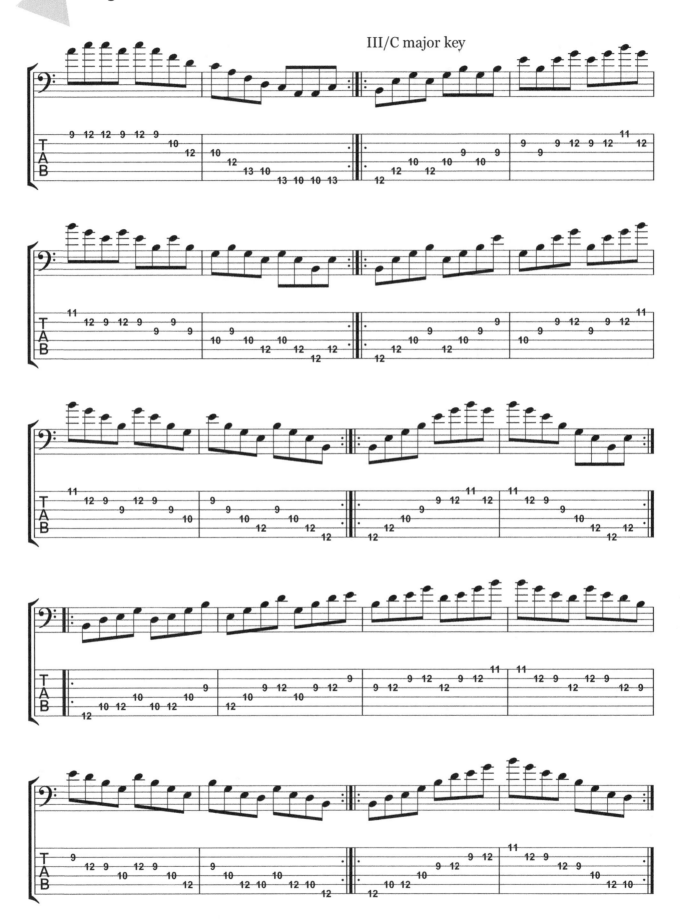

IV/C major key

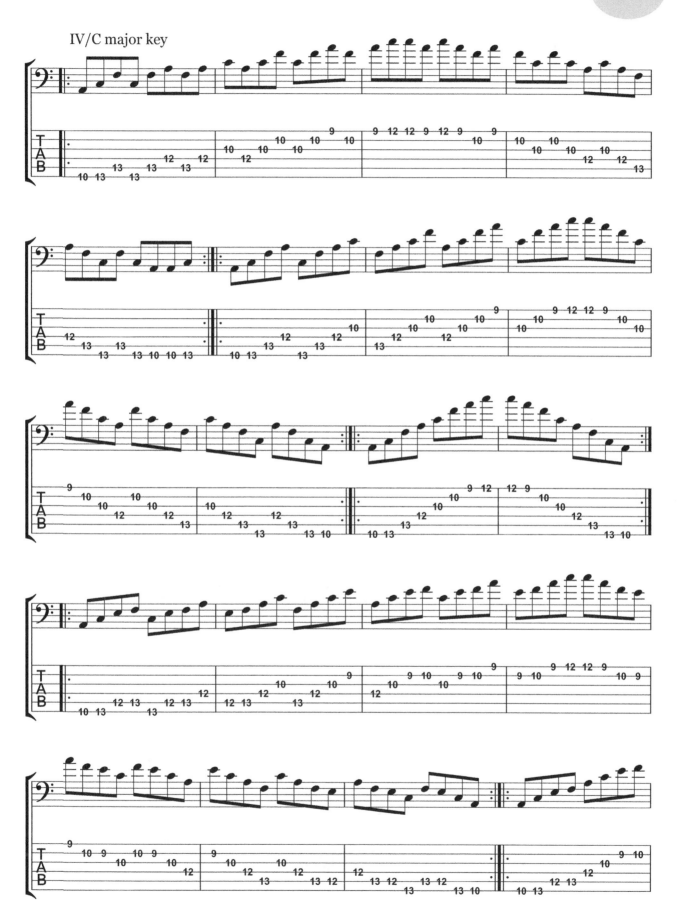

V/C major key

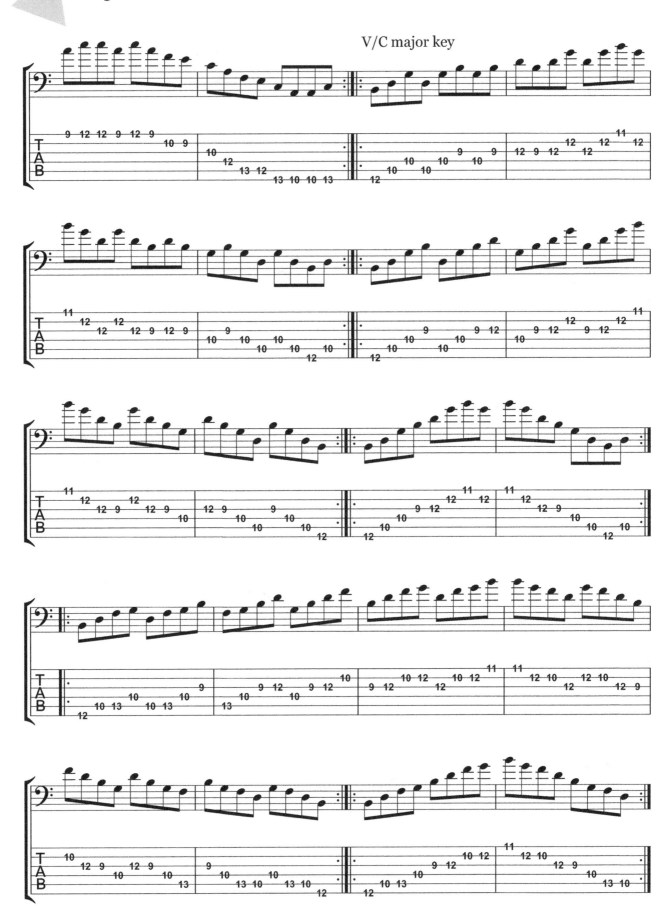

all diatonic arpeggios

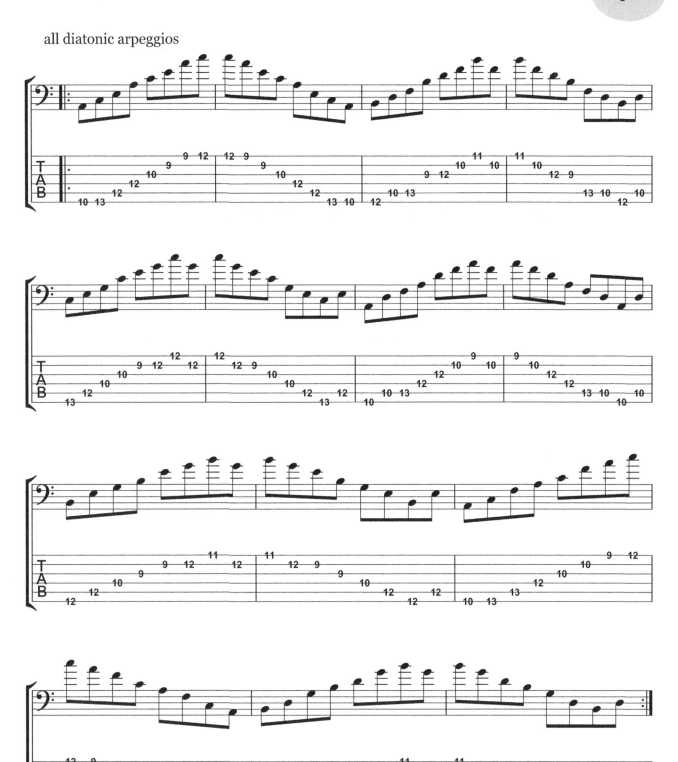

CHAPTER 5

Construction of the diatonic chords in 5 positions

In this chapter we will look at all the diatonic chords that are formed in each separate position. That will help us learn how to use them easily and quickly within any harmonic progression we may come across. We will learn the structure of chords formed on three and four strings.

Position 7-1 chords

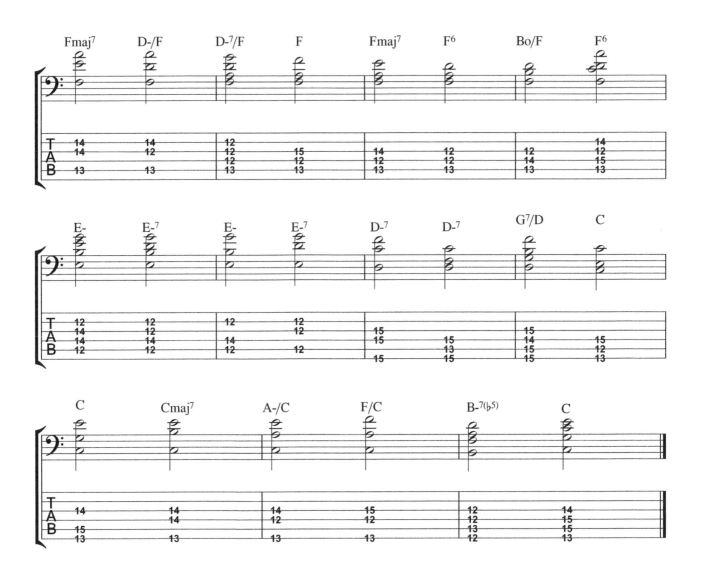

Position 2 chords

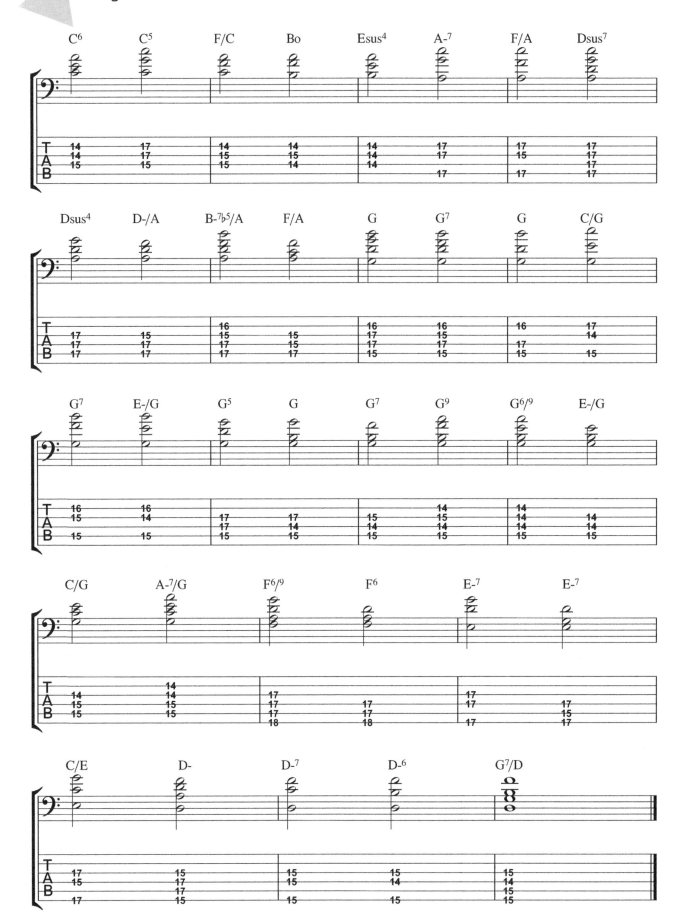

Position 3-4 chords

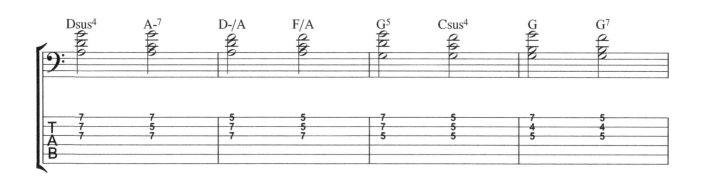

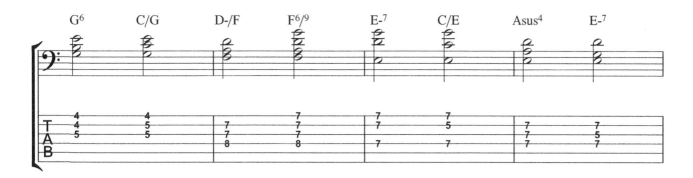

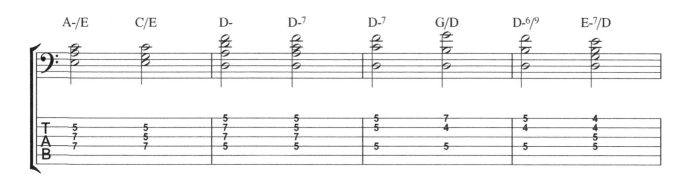

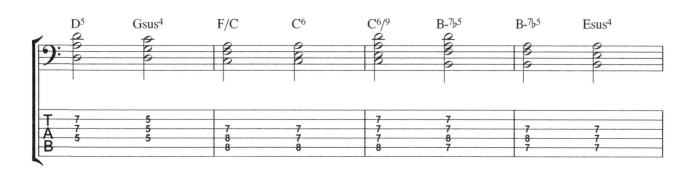

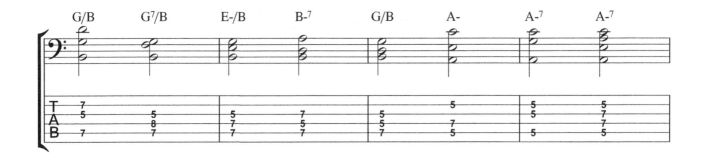

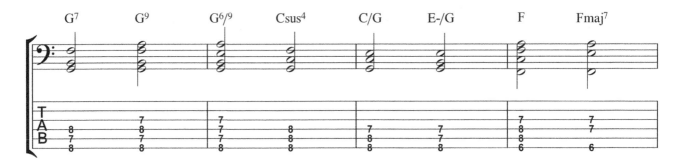

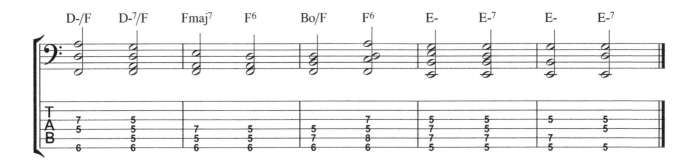

Position 5 chords

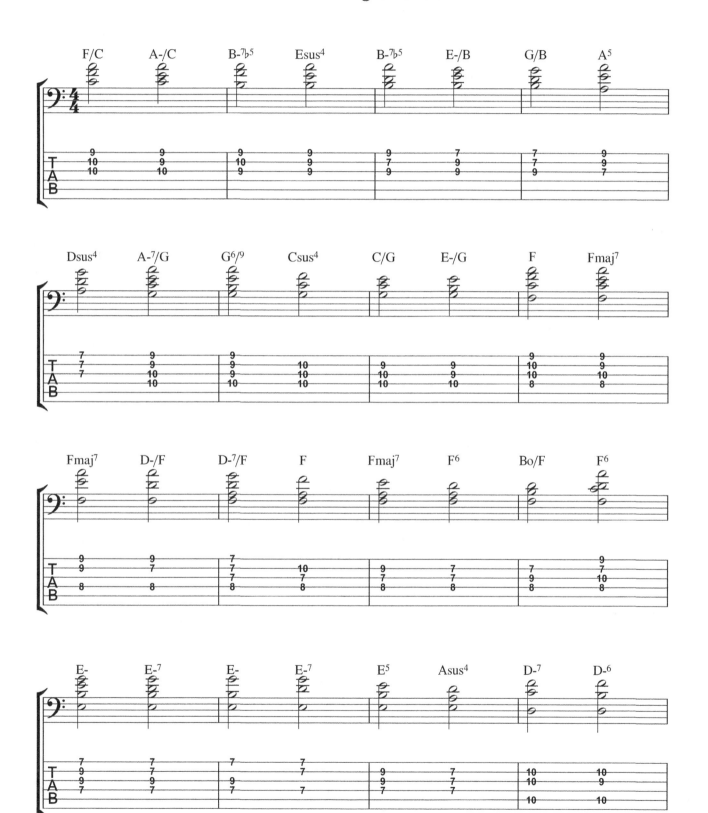

Position 6 chords

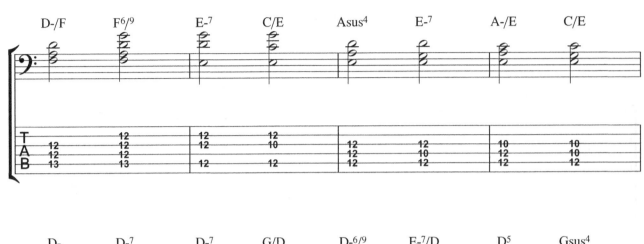

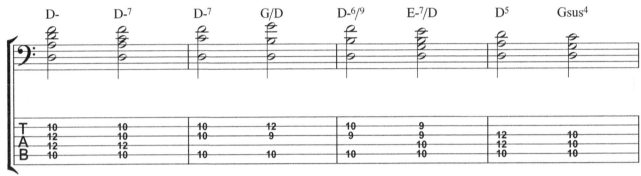

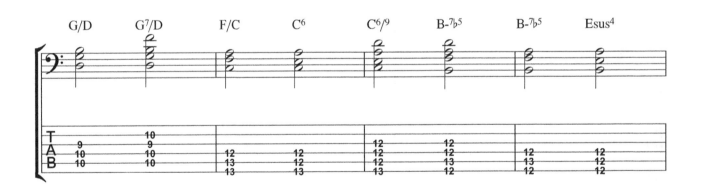

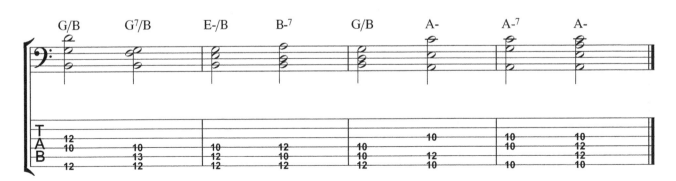

CHAPTER 6

All the positions of the 12 major key centers

The 12 key centers

In this chapter we will examine the position where each key center starts and ends on the fingerboard. This way we will have a complete picture for each key center, and as a result we will be able to use at any time, on any part of the fingerboard, vertically, horizontally, and with ease the notes we need for musical expression when playing a music piece.

Let's examine each key center, one by one, in the order that they appear on the circle of fifths.

Depending on the number of frets that each fingerboard has, each key center ends in a different place. What ensures a safe result is finding the lowest note of each key center on the lowest string of our instrument. In order to find that, we need to figure out what is the first scale degree of each key center (mode) that appears complete at the beginning of the fingerboard. Once we find that scale degree, we automatically find the position where it belongs, and therefore the place where the key center starts.

For example, if we want to find the key center of A major, we see that the lowest diatonic note we can find on the fingerboard is C♯, which is the 3rd degree of A major scale. Therefore, we will play C♯ Phrygian, and the position that starts with the 3rd scale degree is position 3-4. Since we have found the position where the key center starts, we find the remaining positions in their order, Position 5, Position 6, Position 7-1, Position 2, etc. until we cover the entire fingerboard.

C major positions

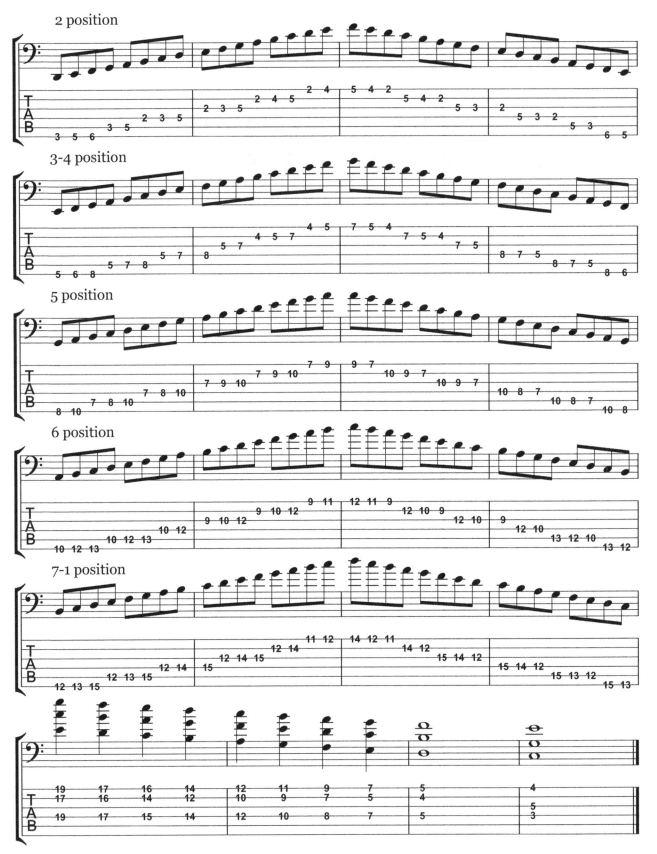

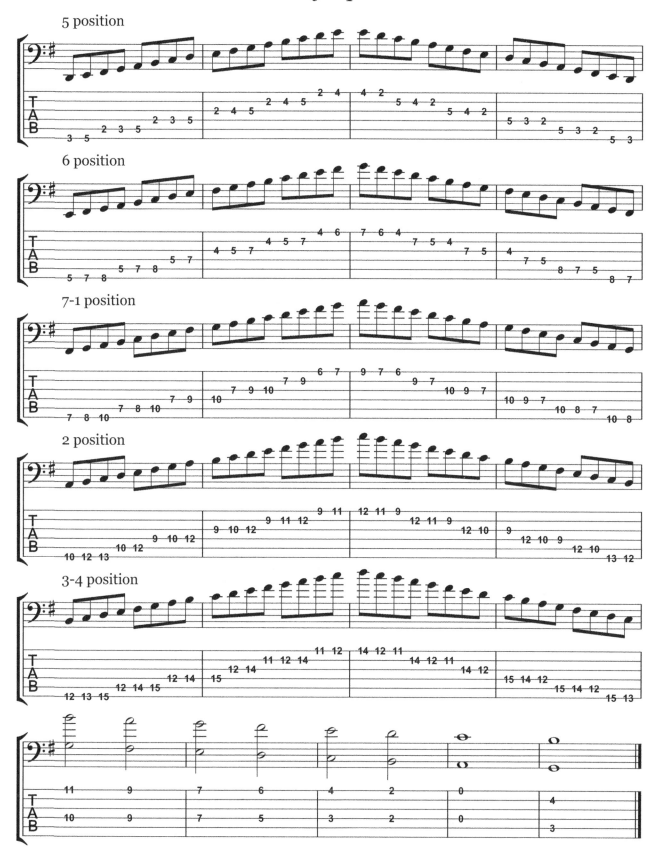

G major positions

D major positions

A major positions

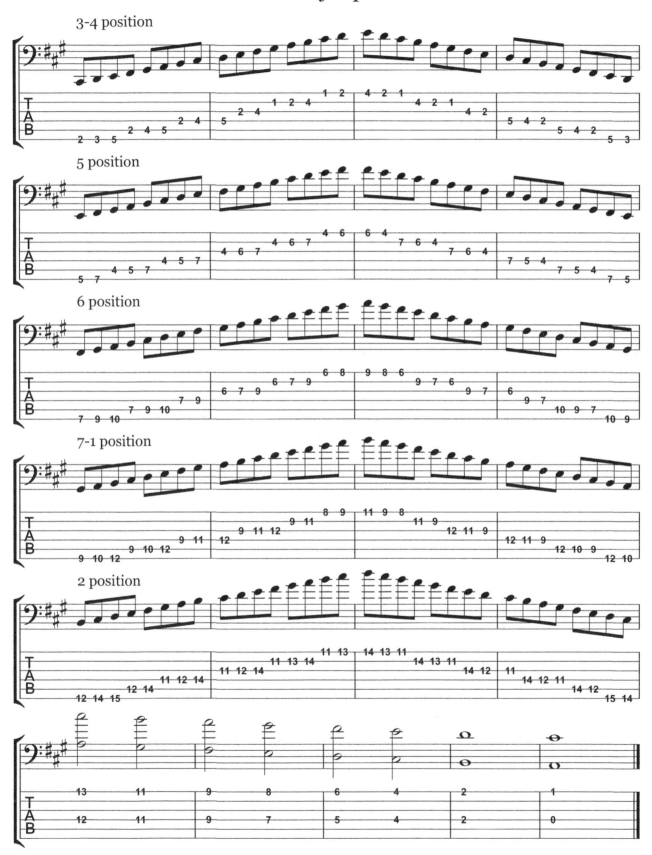

E major positions

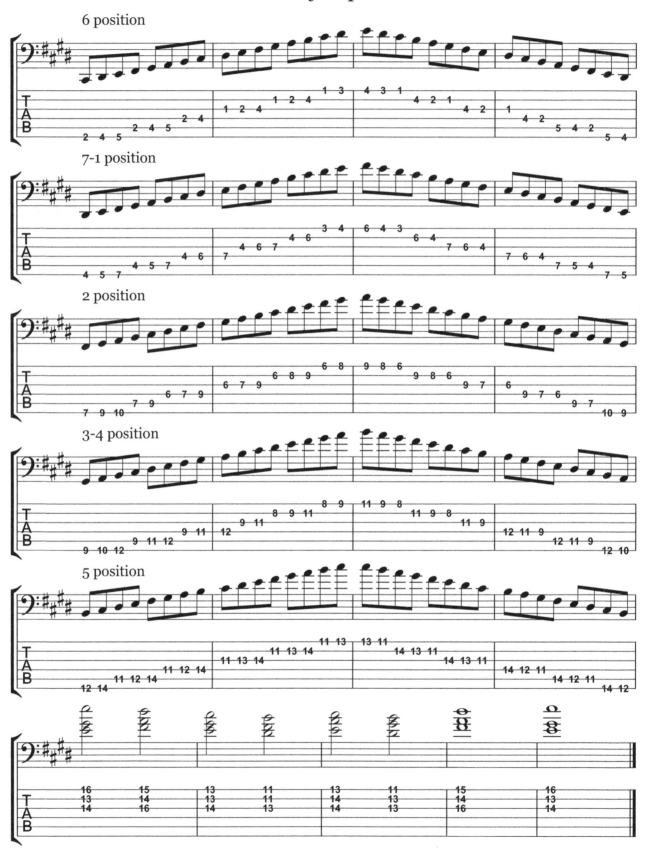

B major positions

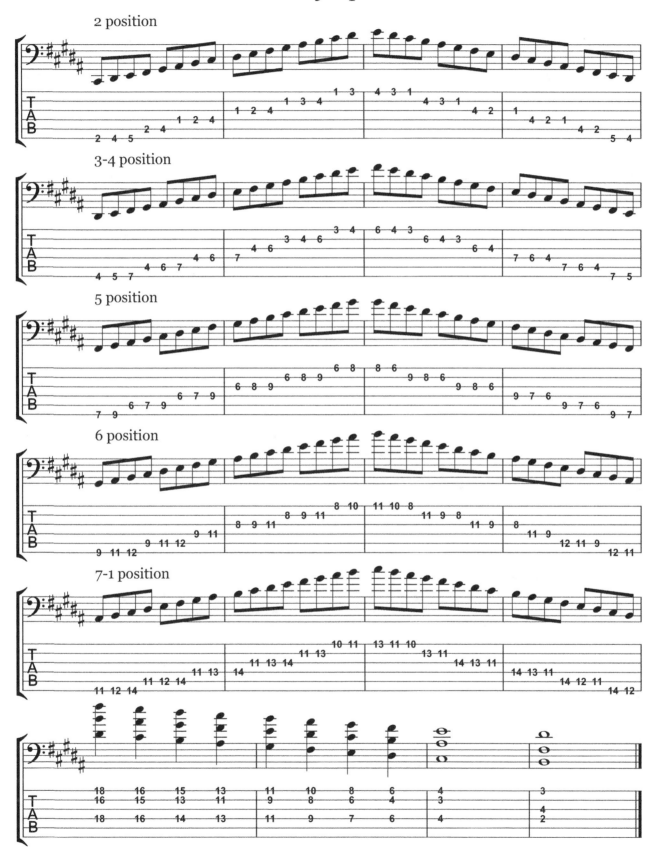

F♯ major positions

C♯ major positions

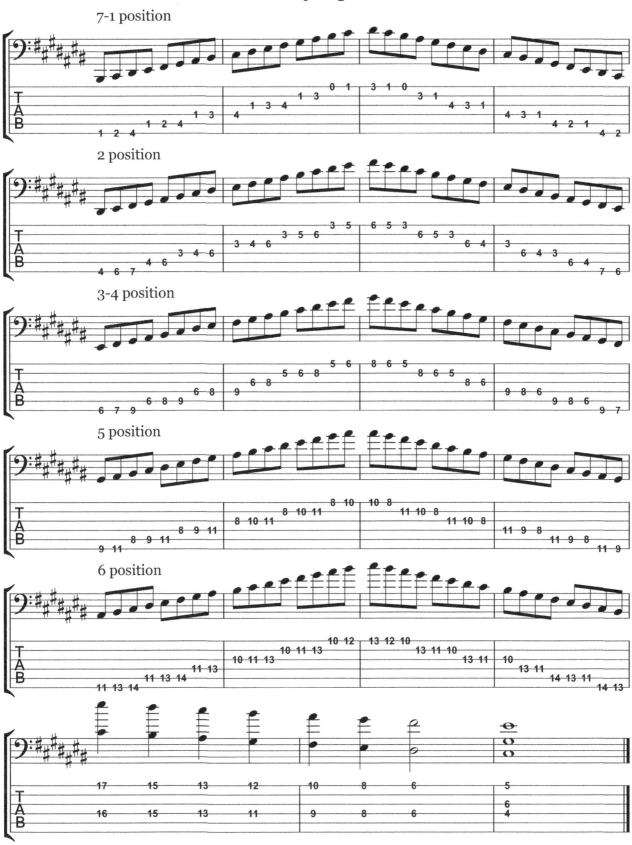

A♭ major positions

E♭ major positions

B♭ major positions

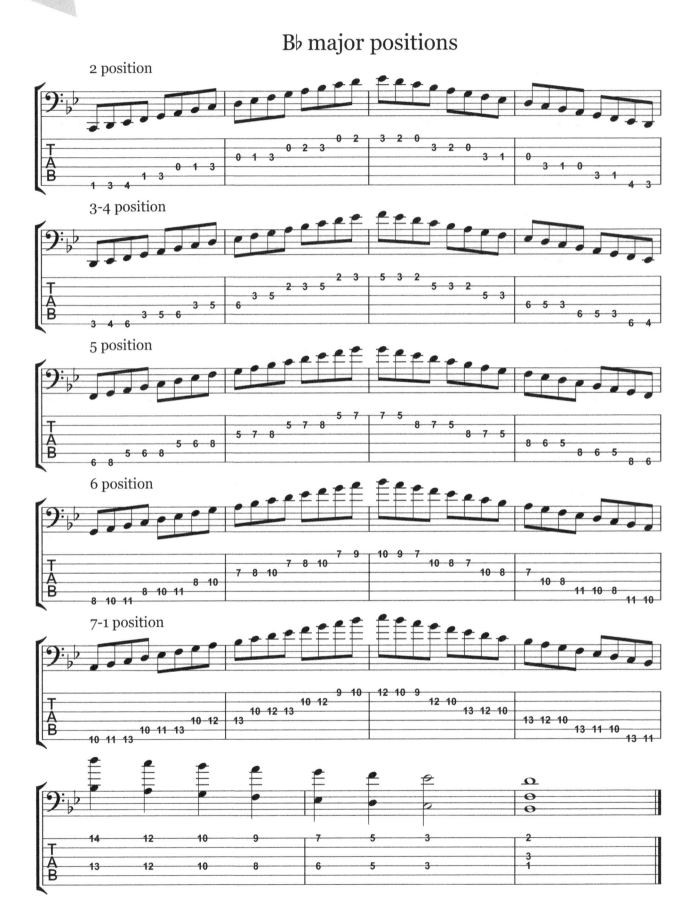

F major positions

CHAPTER 7

Diagonal construction of the modes with tetrachords

The system of the diagonal construction of the modes is based on the symmetrical alternating order of the tetrachords, which are always in a specific order, and it allows us to play every mode diagonally for up to 3 octaves.

This happens as follows:

If we start with the **D Ionian** mode on our lowest string and we play its first tetrachord, we will see that it is a major tetrachord. Then we move with an interval of a major 2nd and we play the second tetrachord of the D Ionian mode which, at the same time, is the first tetrachord of the **A Mixolydian** mode and has a major quality.

We then move again with an interval of a major 2nd in order to play the second tetrachord of A Mixolydian which, at the same time, is the first tetrachord of the **E Dorian** mode and is a minor tetrachord.

Then we move again with an interval of a major 2nd in order to play the second tetrachord of the E Dorian mode which, at the same time, is the first tetrachord of the **B Aeolian** mode and is also a minor tetrachord.

We move again with an interval of a major 2nd and we play the second tetrachord of the B Aeolian mode which is also the first tetrachord of the **F♯ Phrygian** mode and is a Phrygian tetrachord.

From there, we move again with an interval of a major 2nd and we play the second tetrachord of the F♯ Phrygian mode which is also the first tetrachord of the **C♯ Locrian** mode and has a Phrygian quality.

Finally, we move again, but this time with an interval of a minor 2nd, and we play the second tetrachord of the C♯ Locrian mode which is also the first tetrachord of the **G Lydian** mode and is a Lydian tetrachord.

If we move again with an interval of a major 2nd and we play the second tetrachord of the G Lydian mode, we see that it is the first tetrachord of the **D Ionian** mode from which we begun our construction, and we continue in the same way we started.

We clearly see that the construction of the tetrachords follows a specific and repeated order which, starting with the Ionian mode, is:

major- major- minor- minor- phrygian- phrygian- lydian, and then all over again with the same pattern.

A basic requirement in order for the system to work is to maintain with each mode the fingering that we have learned until now. This will happen if we play each beginning tetrachord following the fingering of the new mode it represents. The order of the modes that we find along with the tetrachords is:

Ionian-Mixolydian-Dorian-Aeolian -Phrygian-Locrian-Lydian-Ionian

Of course, we can start from any mode and simply follow the construction order of the tetrachords, and this way we can easily and without much thought play each mode in as many octaves as we desire.

Ionian in 3 octaves with diagonal tetrachords

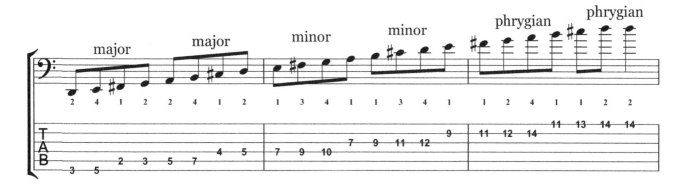

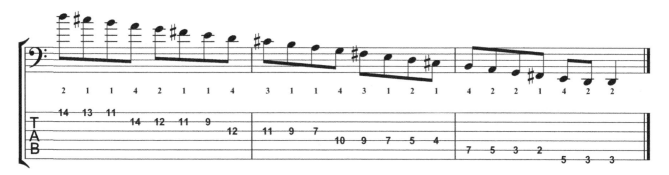

Dorian in 3 octaves with diagonal tetrachords

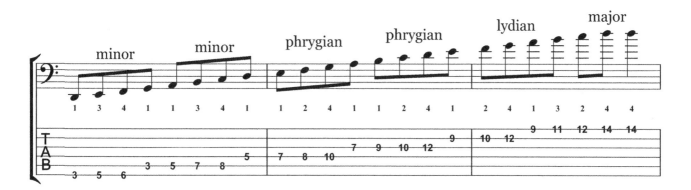

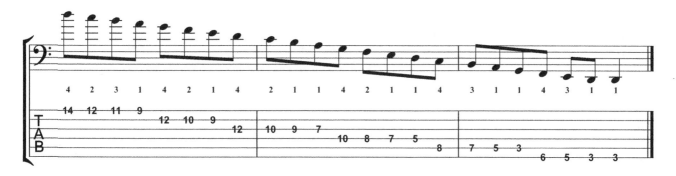

Phrygian in 3 octaves with diagonal tetrachords

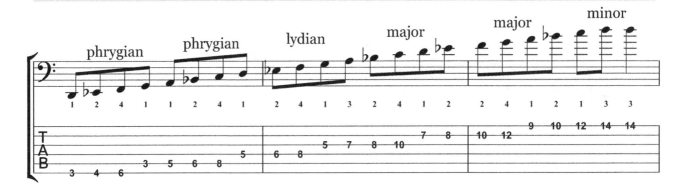

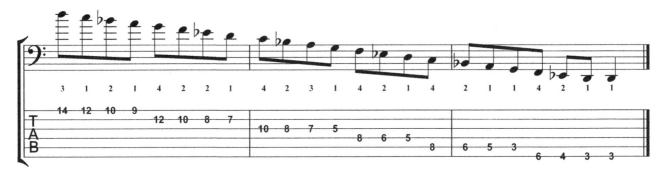

Lydian in 3 octaves with diagonal tetrachords

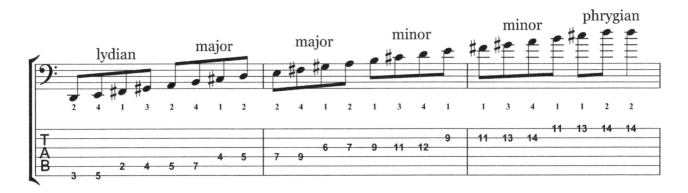

Mixolydian in 3 octaves with diagonal tetrachords

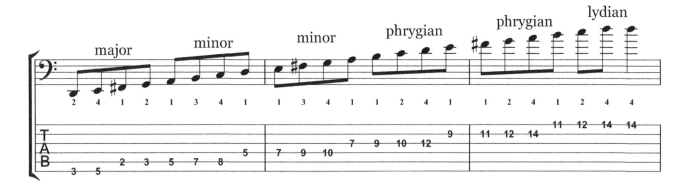

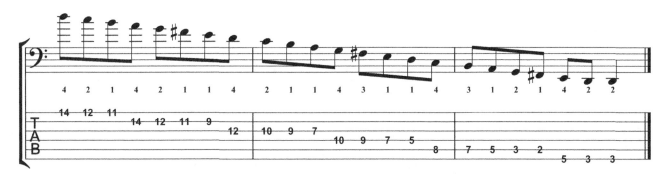

Aeolian in 3 octaves with diagonal tetrachords

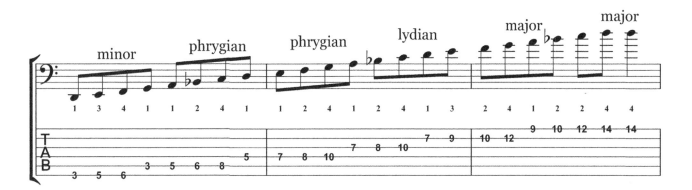

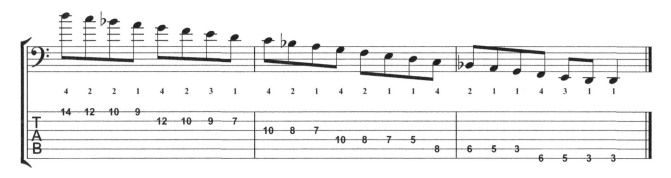

Locrian in 3 octaves with diagonal tetrachords

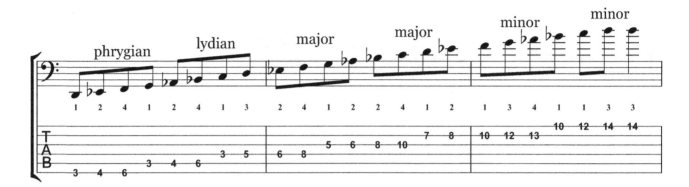

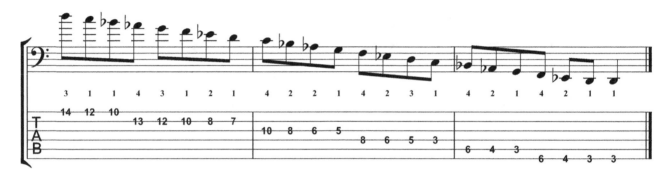

CHAPTER 8 :

Mix positions with F-F♯ System

In the last chapter of the book we will see how we can play in all 12 key centers of the music system while remaining in one position and changing only the manner in which each note develops. That way we will be able to play instantly in any key center without unnecessary movements.

We will examine how we can create melodic and improvisational lines in any key center of our music system based on two notes, F♯ and F. These notes will be the tonic for each of the 7 diatonic modes that we have learned.

Mix positions / F- F♯ system

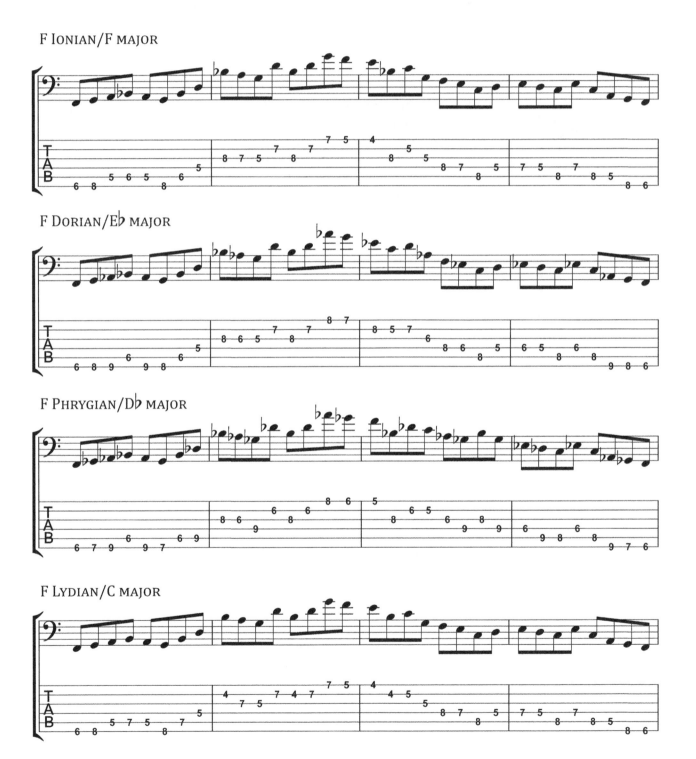

F Mixolydian/B♭ major

F Aeolian/A♭ major

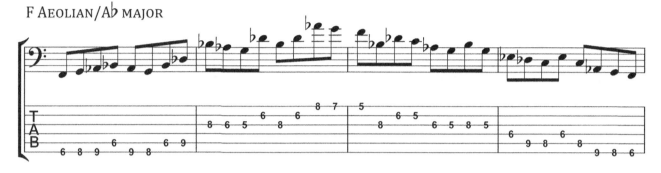

F Locrian/G♭ major

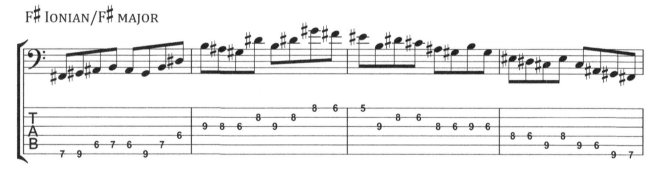

F♯ Ionian/F♯ major

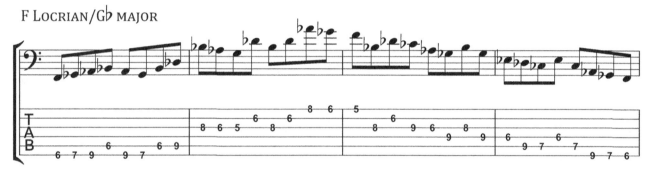

F♯ Dorian/E major

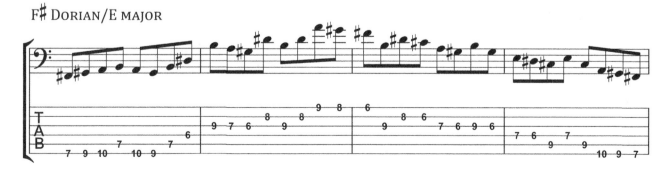

F♯ Phrygian/D major

F♯ Lydian/C♯ major

F♯ Mixolydian/B major

F♯ Aeolian/A major

F♯ Locrian/G major

Epilogue

I want to thank you for the efforts you made to study the first book of the 6 String Bass Guitar, and wish you to continue with the same persistence and placing the acquisition of knowledge advancing the next books in the series.

Petros Dragoumis

Made in the USA
Monee, IL
31 May 2022

97292439R00090